ROUSSEAU AND THE MODERN STATE

ROUSSEAU
AND THE
MODERN STATE

BY
ALFRED COBBAN
Professor of French History
University College, London

ARCHON BOOKS
1964

FIRST PUBLISHED IN 1934

SECOND EDITION 1964

SECOND IMPRESSION 1968

Second Edition © George Allen & Unwin Ltd 1964

ISBN 208 00509 9

PRINTED IN GREAT BRITAIN

by Photolithography

BY NOVELLO & CO. LTD

LONDON, W.I.

268343

TO MURIEL

PREFACE

The second edition of a book I wrote thirty years ago has been completely revised and very largely rewritten. The changes and additions are far too numerous to attempt to indicate them in this preface. The need for such drastic alteration has arisen partly as a result of changes in my own views, not so much on Rousseau as on the whole movement of the Enlightenment, and partly as a result of more recent contributions to the study of Rousseau's political thought, particularly in the writings of Professor Roger Derathé, who has for the first time related Rousseau clearly, and I believe correctly, to his predecessors in the tradition of Natural Law. I have incorporated in this revision material from an article, 'New Light on the Political Thought of Rousseau', which I contributed to the *Political Science Quarterly*, to the editor of which I am grateful for permission to make use of the article in this way.

There have been two main schools of opinion about Rousseau as a political thinker. According to one he should be regarded as a disciple of Locke and the *philosophes*, and the *Contrat social* as the last and greatest of the works of the individualistic school of politics, against which Burke fulminated so effectively that he demolished apparently for ever its intellectual foundations. A later and more influential school of thought has attached Rousseau closely to the German Idealism of the following century, and attempted to make him in part responsible even for the metaphysical madness of its wildest disciples. Between these two extreme and mutually exclusive interpretations students of Rousseau have always been divided. Vaughan, in his valuable edition of Rousseau's *Political Writings*, found it impossible to reconcile the two aspects of Rousseau's political thinking. On the one hand he paid generous testimony to the Rousseau who proclaimed the rights of the individual. More often he saw Rousseau as 'the determined foe of individualism', whose political theory eventuated in a 'communal despotism'. Yet in an Epilogue written after 1914 he adduced all the arguments he could against this conclusion. On the whole, Vaughan seems to have believed that the two strains in

Rousseau's writings cannot be united. 'A stern assertor of the state on the one hand,' he concluded, 'a fiery champion of the individual upon the other, he could never bring himself wholly to sacrifice the one ideal to the other.'

Are we compelled to accept this verdict? Vaughan takes the individual and the state as strictly comparable objects and presents us with the one and the other as alternative ends of social policy on a basis of strict equality. It seems to me that this is a twentieth-century and not an eighteenth-century attitude. Rousseau is primarily a moralist, being, in spite of everything, a child of the Enlightenment. As such Rousseau's end is always the individual and his liberty. It is true that the community has to play an essential part in his liberation; but the state or the community is never more than a means to an end. It never becomes an end in itself. His political theory starts with the individual and it ends with the individual. At the same time Rousseau believes that unless the community is so organized as to endow man with the possibility of moral freedom and liberty he will know neither of these, and that therefore the state necessarily has a certain logical priority to the individual. But this priority is justifiable only in so far as the state does actively develop the individual's moral personality and secure his liberty; while Rousseau can afford to attribute considerable scope to the idea of the state, because he does not allow it any end other than the moral and material well-being and happiness of the individuals who compose it.

Envisaged in this light, it may be suggested, Rousseau's political ideas have no longer to be divided between two violently opposed and irreconcilable extremes. At the very least there is here a *prima facie* case for an attempt to view his political thought as a whole. And if some such interpretation can be substantiated it will compel us to decide that instead of standing at the opposite pole to Burke, Rousseau occupies a position in the history of political theory approximating in many respects to that of his great English antagonist. Such is only to be expected, after all, for one can hardly take Rousseau's literary and social ideas as intimately connected with the early Romantic movement, and leave his political ideas on one side as though they belonged to an alien current of thought.

The truth, it seems to me, is that Rousseau's is in the modern

world still one of the most complete attempts to discuss the
basic problem presented by all states, but in a peculiarly acute
form by the modern state—that of the relationship between
the individual and the community. The problem in its simplest
form is to safeguard the liberty of the individual, while at the
same time giving the state the moral authority and actual
power which it needs if it is to function effectively for the
benefit of the individuals composing it. While it would not be
true to say that Rousseau examines this problem in all its
theoretical and practical implications, nevertheless one cannot
help being surprised to find the many angles from which he
approaches it. Because of its intrinsic importance, as well as on
account of Rousseau's evident preoccupation with it, I found
myself concentrating my attention on this problem. It still
seems to me by no means an unprofitable standpoint from
which to make a survey of Rousseau's political theory.

In conclusion, I must repeat here the thanks expressed in the
preface to the first edition to the Rockefeller Foundation for the
grant of a Fellowship which enabled me to work in France on
certain historical problems and incidentally gave me the leisure
for the completion of this book; to my friend, Mr. R. S. Elmes,
for his generosity in permitting me to use and print extracts
from the manuscripts of the comte d'Antraigues; and to the
Research Committee of Armstrong College, now the University
of Newcastle upon Tyne, for a grant in aid of publication.

The following are the editions of Rousseau to which I have
referred.

Political Writings of Rousseau, ed. C. E. Vaughan, 2 vols., Cambridge,
     1915.
La Nouvelle Héloïse, ed. D. Mornet, 4 vols., Paris, 1925.
Les Confessions, suivie des Rêveries d'un Promeneur solitaire, ed. A. van
     Bever, 3 vols., Paris, 1927.
Correspondence Générale, ed. T. Dufour, Paris, 1924-34.
Œuvres, ed. du Peyrou, Geneva, 1782.

ALFRED COBBAN

University College, London
February, 1964

CONTENTS

CHAPTER I

THE INTERPRETATION OF ROUSSEAU

1. THE STUDY OF THE POLITICAL THEORY OF ROUSSEAU

Political thinkers of the past, who normally believed in the practical importance of their ideas, and wished to convert their contemporaries to their own beliefs, wrote to be understood. With a few exceptions they were masters of style. It has to be asked, indeed, why they need explaining at all. Can they not be left to say what they mean without the interposition of a commentator? Why, in particular, should we occupy ourselves with a writer such as Jean Jacques Rousseau, whole political writings are comparatively small in bulk and lucid in style? If the object were simply to provide a *précis* of them, it would be difficult to find any satisfactory answer. Some political philosophers require to be rewritten before they can be understood, though even then the proceeding must give rise to doubts, since between an idea as explained by a later critic and the same idea as adumbrated in the terms of the original writer, there may be a world of difference.[1] That a thinker has not been understood in his own day is of course no proof of lack of clarity, it may indicate no more than the originality of his ideas; and this, one may suggest,

---

[1] Because of the importance of basing any discussion on the exact words of Rousseau, I have quoted him always from the original French and not in translation. The dangers of the latter are illustrated in 'Rousseau's *Du Contrat Social*: some problems of translation', by J. H. Burns and A. Cobban, *Political Studies*, X. ii. (1962) 203-7. To take the translation most commonly used in this country, in that by G. D. H. Cole in Everyman's Library some major terms are fundamentally altered in passing from French to English. Thus *corps moral* is translated as 'moral body' and *personne moral* as 'moral person'; in fact what these terms meant in the eighteenth century was an artificial, hypothetical entity, which lawyers would call a '*persona ficta*'. *Mœurs* becomes 'manners', 'morals', 'morality'; customs or patterns of social behaviour would be nearer the meaning. *Ordre* is rendered 'class', but of course Rousseau has the *ancien régime* orders of society in mind, not the later economic classes. *Droit* is naturally an ambiguous word. Cole translates it as 'legal right' where 'equality before the law' is the obvious meaning; for *toujours droit*, 'rightful' would be better than 'always in the right'.

is in part the explanation of the inability of his contemporaries to understand the political ideas of Rousseau. By itself it is not a justification for a restatement of them, now that many of what were considered startling paradoxes have become the commonplaces of politics.

One objection to these very reasonable doubts is that words change their meaning and that ideas do not exist in isolation but take on their particular significance from the world of thought to which they belong. Thus Hobbes, for example, begins, 'Nature, the Art whereby God hath made and governs the world', but this simple and lucid phrase means something very different now from what it meant when Hobbes wrote it. Rousseau is much nearer to us than Hobbes, but even he lived and wrote in a very different world of thought from ours. The first duty of the student of Rousseau's political thought, it seems to me, is to attempt to rediscover its original intention across the barrier interposed by the many and varying interpretations, often of a polemical character, which have obscured it, and to put it back in its eighteenth-century setting.

A modern study of Rousseau's ideas cannot follow exactly the arrangement that he himself adopted. The points which seem critical to one age, the subjects around which controversy wages, are not always those which in the light of subsequent development appear the most vital. Ideas that were taken for granted and therefore not emphasized are likely to be more important for the comprehension of their own times. Those which were most original are the most likely to have remained unremarked. New tendencies appear as single spies more often than in big battalions. Rousseau's theories were fated to become closely linked with the most violent political dissensions: bearing this in mind, it is easy to understand why the studies of his political theory which do not start from a definitely revolutionary or anti-revolutionary standpoint are still few.

From one frequent cause of misinterpretation Rousseau is comparatively free: literary controversy was not natural to him and he therefore escaped the temptation it offered for the distortion of his ideas. The joy of wordy battle for its own sake, regardless of the ultimate value of the ideas over the dead bodies of which the fight was waged, passed him by almost completely: if he said a thing it was because he believed it intensely.

Intellectual agnosticism, suspension of judgment, the scepticism of an Erasmus or an Anatole France, did not come into the scope of his mind; it was not a characteristic, anyhow, of those positive, dogmatic, denunciatory spirits of the eighteenth century. Yet even with Rousseau a certain literary love of paradox may be suspected in his earlier writings and has certainly not been without influence on the interpretation of his ideas. It accounts for the attention lavished on the idea of an historical state of nature, which, looked at in perspective, seems to us out of proportion even to the part it played in eighteenth-century thought. Considered as an element of historical significance in relation to the subsequent development of ideas, it in no way deserves the emphasis it has obtained, and if Rousseau is given his due place in the general current of European thought it sinks almost to insignificance.

I must make it clear that in undertaking a study of Rousseau's political ideas, my object is a strictly limited one. My intention is not to relate him to individual thinkers who preceded or followed him; or to trace generally his origins and influences. The danger inherent in this line of approach is the tendency to stress unduly those aspects in which the influence of the past is shown, and by linking a theorist too closely with his predecessors to obscure his real originality. For Rousseau particularly, old and accepted ideas such as the social contract and natural rights provide a formal framework for his thought rather than anything more essential. If, on the other hand, we attempt to link Rousseau too closely with his successors this inevitably means associating him with the Idealist philosophers, and therefore emphasizing those aspects of his thought which can be reconciled with their ideas, and neglecting other elements or at least treating them as contradictory instead of possibly complementary.

If we set Rousseau in an academic, or mainly theoretic tradition we necessarily fail to do justice to him, but as a prophet of ideas destined to have a great future one can hardly exaggerate his significance. In politics, in ethics, in literature, in social customs, one finds him, says Lanson, at the entrance to all avenues leading to the present. 'J.-J. Rousseau,' reflects Amiel, 'est un ancêtre en tout: il a créé le voyage à pied avant Töpffer, la rêverie avant René, la botanique littéraire avant George Sand, le culte de la nature avant Bernardin de Saint-Pierre, la théorie démocratique avant la révolution de 1789, la discussion politique et la discussion théologique avant Mirabeau et Renan, la pédagogie avant restalozzi, la peinture des Alpes avant de Saussure: il a mis la musique à la mode et éveillé le goût des confessions au public; il a fait un nouveau style français, le style serré, châtié, dense, passionné. En somme, on peut dire que rien de Rousseau ne s'est perdu et que personne n'a influé plus que lui, sur la Révolution française, . . . et sur le XIXme siècle.'[1] It is true that on many points one can find anticipators of Rousseau, that on others his generation was clearly coming of itself to attitudes that were perhaps most plainly manifested in his writings, but hardly anywhere do we find assembled in the ideas of one man so many new tendencies, so much of the intellectual furniture of a later age. In a general sense, without necessarily accepting any particular interpretation of his influence, it is clear that this was enormous, that Bergson was not unreasonable in claiming that Rousseau's was the most powerful of the influences which the human mind has experienced since Descartes.[2] It is true that the deepest influences are often only to be remarked at long range. In the development of literature, in many phases of social life, and in educational theory, Rousseau's influence over his contemporaries is well marked. In other fields, particularly in politics, his immediate influence is more a matter for debate and has been unduly magnified. At any rate, it is with his political ideas in themselves, and not with their historical effects, that I am concerned.

This is not a suitable place in which to discuss the vexed question of the influence of political theory over political practice. Can it be said that without Rousseau there would have been no ideas such as democracy or nationalism, or even that the form these took would have been different in any way had he not lived? This is not to imply that political theory is without practical bearing. Its effect naturally depends on the extent to which its ideas are diffused, especially among the directing elements of society. While the systematic study of political life remains esoteric, a mystery of the academies or of a narrow literary circle, its influence is necessarily negligible. It might be

[1] Amiel, *Fragments d'un journal intime*, 5th ed., 1877, i. 219.
[2] H. Bergson, *La Philosophie* in *La Science Française*, 1915, p. 21.

claimed for Rousseau that he made an important contribution
to the growth of a general interest in political ideas, which was
to introduce a new factor into history of which we are far as yet
from seeing all the consequences.

The political ideas of Rousseau, moreover, throw a valuable
light on the origins of many of the fundamental political ideas
of the nineteenth century and of the present day, and are of
great aid in the comprehension of those ideas, quite apart from
any influence he may or may not have exercised. The ideas in
which the historian is most interested are not recondite academic
doctrines, to be traced with great labour from one obscure
theorist to another; they are the truths of the market-place, the
battle cries of the peoples. Yet these general conceptions, that
play such a great part in history, are those most in need of the
conscious analysis and illustration that only the genius who
understands and shares them can provide. Rousseau is worth
studying, if only because in him can be clearly seen for the first
time so many of our own accepted ideas, and because the essential nature of an idea is often most manifest in its beginnings.

One of the reasons why we may claim that he helps us to
understand the fundamental political ideas of our world, is that
in these we have at bottom progressed very little beyond him
and his contemporaries. Our political thinking is still largely set
in the same terms. Not that Rousseau comprehends the whole
of the political thought even of his own day; but if to him we
add the greatest of his contemporaries in this field, Burke and
Bentham, it will be a little difficult to say in what respects we
have advanced in political ideas, save in a greater awareness of
the complexity and the difficulty of organising political institutions.

Even if the study of governmental machinery has developed
greatly, by itself this tells little of the real means by which men
are governed. It tells us how to organise government, but not
how to create, or even how to maintain a political régime. It is
a subject of constant complaint that too great attention is paid
to institutions as such, and too little to the political habits and
traditions which are necessary to work and uphold them. Of the
importance of this element in politics Burke is the greatest
exponent. The practical value of Bentham's doctrines derives
from the fact that he had seized upon one very important

B

element in the make-up of man as a political animal, the self-interest motive and, applying it systematically, was able to draw from it practical conclusions of incalculable value. Rousseau, on the other hand, has often been regarded as the arch-priest of abstract political theory, based on logic and ignoring human nature and practical utility, though if he were truly this one would be at a loss to explain the importance which he undoubtedly retains for the modern student of political thought. The fact is that Rousseau and Burke and Bentham emphasize different aspects of political life; but for this very reason they are the more worth studying, because they supplement one another. For the modern student of politics they have all three to be reckoned with in a way that no subsequent thinker on politics has, and certainly not least Rousseau, who among friends and enemies alike is taken by general agreement as the true prophet, if not the very source and fountain-head of the modern democratic state.

One consideration of a different nature remains to be discussed before we can leave these preliminaries. It is sometimes said that Rousseau's political writings present a mass of contradictions to which chronology affords the only key. This is a serious charge, because if Rousseau is as self-contradictory as is alleged one cannot help wondering if he is worth studying. For how are we to know which of any particular pair of opposed ideas to choose as expressive of his real thought? Is it possible to find historical significance in a writer of such inconsistency? In this respect he is his own most severe critic, for he confesses that though he can apprehend individual truths clearly he cannot compare them or arrange them with method, that reverie is more natural to him than reflection, and so forth—all of which sounds a very strange self-criticism from the author of the *Contrat social*.

It has been by taking isolated statements and contrasting them with one another that his critics have most easily established the inconsistency of Rousseau. Against this all too easy method of pulling an author to pieces he himself protested, above all against the habit of judging a book from scattered fragments, picked out by a dishonest critic, who himself is the author of the evil he is criticizing, by isolating a statement from all that modifies and develops it, and twisting it from its true meaning.[1] Thus,

[1] *Œuvres*, vi. 152: *Lett. Mont.* I.

the Second Discourse, interpreted as an expression of the extremist individualism, is used to contradict all his subsequent works. Even among the latter however it is a simple matter to contrast, for instance, the abstract *Contrat social* with the detailed and practical *Poland*, its authoritarian principles with the liberal ideas of the *Lettres de la Montagne*, or its apparent submission of the individual to society with the essential individualism of the *Emile*. But when we reflect that the *Discours sur l'inégalité* and the *Economie politique* came within eighteen months of one another, and that the *Emile* and the *Contrat social* are almost contemporary, we are compelled to examine the alleged inconsistency a little more closely instead of taking it for granted.

The manner in which Vaughan disposes of the difficulty is convincing at first sight. The individualism of Rousseau, he says, is to be found only in the Second Discourse and the first few chapters of the *Contrat social*. Strike these out and it will be seen to be a myth. His explanation is that Rousseau, beginning as a follower of Locke and therefore an extreme individualist, in the critical years, and especially when he was writing the *Contrat social*, was a wholehearted disciple of Plato; only to fall subsequently, when he produced his constitution for Poland, under the influence of Montesquieu.[1] It is difficult to accept this view. The individualism of Rousseau is hardly as limited as Vaughan suggests. The influence of Plato must be admitted, thought he is rarely mentioned by Rousseau; but to confine it to one particular stage in the growth of his mind, and to attribute to it such a decisive influence, is little more than surmise. On the other hand the influence of Montesquieu, far from being confined to the *Poland*, is written large over all his political works.

The most reasonable way of treating the political thought of Rousseau, then, is not to assume that it presents a mass of irreconcilable inconsistencies, nor to attempt to escape from this assumed difficulty by imposing on him an arbitrary scheme of development, for which there is little evidence, but rather to study his works as a whole, and disengage what fundamental unity one can. His importance in the history of thought does not lie in any attempt at an impossible completeness and finality. His originality derives from his intensely personal approach to

[1] Vaughan, *Political Writings of Rousseau*, i. 77-81.

the problems of society. One of his greatest virtues as a political thinker is that he was not a system-maker.

2. ROUSSEAU AND THE FRENCH REVOLUTION

The interpretation of Rousseau throughout the greater part of the nineteenth century suffered, as has already been suggested, from the fact that he was viewed through the mists of the revolutionary age. His name was inevitably associated with the revolution, both with the popular disorders in which it began, and the excess of governmental authority in which it ended. For both these developments in turn he has been made chiefly responsible. This identification of Rousseau with the revolution has naturally prevailed most strongly in France, where indeed his name has become, as for many it still remains, a political war-cry. But though he has always been in the centre of the battle, it is not in his name that either party fights. The one point on which most political opinions have concurred is hostility to Jean-Jacques. For enemies of the revolution he is identified with all its works; those in the revolutionary tradition have inherited the prejudices of the *philosophes* against him; while for liberals he is the chief author of that worship of the state which has been the greatest menace to liberalism during the last century. So that in sum we are forced to agree with Beaulavon that it is difficult to find anyone in France who in politics can be reckoned an heir to Rousseau.[1]

It seems evident that the *Contrat social* was little read before 1789,[2] and that it had little influence on the opening phases of the revolution.[3] Indeed, Rousseau seems to have been quoted more often on the counter-revolutionary than on the revolutionary side. Against this, it is alleged that even if ignored in the early years of the Revolution, the *Contrat social* came into

---

[1] G. Beaulavon, *Contrat social*, ed. 1903 (2nd ed. 1914), p. 94.

[2] D. Mornet, 'Les enseignements des bibliothèques privées (1750-80)', in *Revue d'histoire littéraire de la France*, 1910.

[3] The political influence of Rousseau before the revolution and in its opening stages is discussed, on the basis of an extensive documentation, by Mrs Joan Macdonald in a forthcoming book, to be published by the University of London, Athlone Press.

power with the Jacobins.[1] Mallet du Pan relates that Marat was
reading and commenting on it to enthusiastic street-corner
audiences in 1788.[2] Considering the difficulty which modern
University students find in following the concise and complicated argument of Rousseau's major political treatise, this sup-
poses a remarkable degree of philosophical grasp and political
sophistication in the Parisian populace. It is surprising that anyone has ever taken such a silly statement as this of Mallet du
Pan seriously. The system of Robespierre has also been taken as
the *Contrat social* put into practical politics. As this charge is
usually based neither on an attempt to comprehend the political
philosophy of Rousseau, nor on an analysis of the political practice of Robespierre, we may at least suspend judgment, only
observing that his influence was not needed, as has been alleged,
to develop an idea of governmental despotism, which could be
learnt in full from the *ancien régime*.[3] On the other hand, in
1802 we find a constitutional *curé* denouncing Rousseau to
Bonaparte as the source of all the ills of France. 'Tous les
anarchistes sont ses partisans, tous les ennemis de l'ordre
invoquent ses principes.'[4] Both extreme views are historically
unjustifiable. Even a slight acquaintance with revolutionary
literature is enough to show that the political influence of
Rousseau is by no means clear and simple. Quite apart from the
plain fact that reference to the authority of Rousseau, whose
literary arts had moved a whole generation to tears, rapidly
became a commonplace of revolutionary oratory, and that the
vast majority of such references are the merest generalities, more
often than not devoid of meaning, one would have to neglect the
influence he exercised over the younger *noblesse*, on the Catholic
Revival and on thinkers such as Chateaubriand and Bonald,

[1] A. Meynier, *Jean-Jacques Rousseau révolutionnaire*, 1912, p. 125; L. Duguit,
Rousseau, Kant et Hegel, 1918, p. 6. On the other side is Beaulavon, *op. cit.*,
pp. 80, 81, 94, who quotes Chateaubriand to the effect that no book condemns
the Terrorists more than the *Contrat social*. Even Vaughan, however, allows
that 'the later and more terrible phases' of the revolution saw the triumph of
the fundamental ideas of the *Contrat social*. (*Political Writings*, intro., i. 21-2.)

[2] Mallet du Pan, *Mémoires*, 1851, i. 126 n.

[3] I have discussed the political ideas of Robespierre and considered his rela-
tion to Rousseau in two articles—'The Fundamental Ideas of Robespierre',
English Historical Review, 1948, lxiii. 29-51; 'The Political Ideas of Maximilien
Robespierre during the Period of the Convention', *id.*, 1946, lxi. 45-80.

[4] P.-M. Masson, *La Religion de Rousseau*, 1916, iii. 257.

Wordsworth and Coleridge and the German idealists, if one wished to accept the older theory of his revolutionary influence. Had the counter-revolution triumphed in 1790, would it not have been partly in the name of Rousseau, with *mandats impératifs*, opposition to the representative system, federalism, and the principle of an independent executive?[1] The authority Rousseau attributes to the king in his *Poland* would have been recalled, and the conservative influence his writings are allowed to have exercised in the early years of the nineteenth century, with the Catholic Revival and German idealism, would have been ante-dated by twenty or more years.

In a more general way one might perhaps be tempted to attribute to Rousseau the blame for the dangerous habit of discussing political questions in terms of the broadest generalizations, and imagining that the whole matter was settled when a sufficiently comprehensive definition had been found. But this verbalism and faith in formulae, from which not even Montesquieu is free, and which is translated into practice in the form of an undue belief in the efficacy of laws and declarations of rights, is characteristic of the whole century: indeed, in his writings on Geneva, Corsica and Poland, Rousseau himself escapes as far from it as any contemporary French writer. We can describe his influence best in the words Faguet uses to describe the general effect of the philosophical writings of the whole century. 'Elles ont traversé toute la Révolution française comme des projections de phares, et c'est à leurs lumières intermittentes qu'on a combattu dans les ténèbres. Leurs livres ont été les textes dont se sont appuyés les partis pour soutenir les revendications diverses et contraires qui leur étaient inspirées par leurs passions ou leurs intérêts.'[2]

3. THE CRITICS OF ROUSSEAU

While the revolutionaries were lauding Rousseau to the skies, it was natural that their enemies should equally vehemently denounce the author who was supposed to be the source of so much mischief. The chorus of denunciation begins with Burke,

[1] cf. Appendix I.

[2] E. Faguet, *La politique comparée de Montesquieu, Rousseau et Voltaire*, 1902, p. 280.

who, after a comparatively moderate criticism in the *Reflections,* launches an attack in the most unmeasured language in his *Letter to a Member of the National Assembly.* His criticism is worth pausing over, because even where he is most violent Burke is never without reason, and because he sets the note, and indeed sums up most of what was to be said on the same subject subsequently. If, as seems highly probable, we can take the book reviews in the earlier years of the *Annual Register* as the work of Burke, his reaction to Rousseau thirty years before the French Revolution anticipates some of the criticisms he was to make later. A review of Rousseau's *Letter to d'Alembert* in 1759 says that his 'tendency to paradox, which is always the bane of solid learning, and threatens now to destroy it, a splenetic disposition carried to misanthropy, and an austere virtue pursued to an unsociable fierceness, have prevented a great deal of the good effects which might be expected from such a genius'. Another review, in 1762, discusses *Emile,* which is criticised on the ground that it has 'some very considerable parts that are impracticable, others that are Chimerical; and not a few highly blameable, and dangerous both to piety and morals'. 'However,' the reviewer continues, 'with those faults in the design, with the whimsies into which his paradoxical genius continually hurries him, there are a thousand noble hints relating to the subject, grounded upon a profound knowledge of the human mind, and the order of its operation.'[1] The political passions aroused by the revolution prevented Rousseau from being envisaged by Burke, after 1789, as merely paradoxical, and if a genius then as a wholly evil one.

Burke's procedure is to take Rousseau as the embodiment of the political philosophy of the revolution. What this was in his opinion he sums up succinctly and clearly. The revolution begins as a revolt of the individual against the bonds with which for his own good he is shackled by the institutions of society: it is an outburst of egoism on a nationwide scale. This is only the first step, it does not represent the real end of the revolution. The selfish passions thus evoked are used by the small conspiracy of ambitious men who have called them forth for the destruction of the existing forces of social control. But their ultimate object is not anarchy, or the abolition of all authority, but merely the

[1] Thomas W. Copeland, *Edmund Burke, Six Essays,* 1950, pp. 136-9.

turning out of office of the existing and traditional authorities, whom they aim at replacing by themselves. When the new illegitimate rule has been established, however, it is bound by none of the customary restrictions that made the former despotism tolerable; the new rulers having freed themselves from the prejudices of moral law, following rapidly on the heels of the initial anarchy, instead of freedom comes the most ruthless and complete dictatorship. This, according to Burke, is exactly the process prepared and prophesied in the works of Rousseau: he first lets loose the unregulated passions of the individual, and then sacrifices him to the tyranny of the state: such is the result of the abandonment of moral law and the divorce of politics from ethics. With what justice this description can be applied to Rousseau we shall see later. Its applicability to the revolution is more plausible—but fair or not it embodies the verdict of the nineteenth century on Rousseau, and the schools of thought which we will have rapidly to survey for the most part merely repeat in different language different parts of Burke's thesis.

This is eminently true of the most influential of the early enemies of the revolutionary philosophy in France, the theocrats, though here we have to reckon with another factor, the influence of Rousseau himself; for writers such as Bonald and de Maistre belonged to the generation that had experienced most fully his fascination. Both Bonald and de Maistre begin with Rousseau. Not only do they acknowledge the justice of many of his views in themselves, but the practical problem as they envisage it is posited in similar terms. Their criticism follows the line of attack taken up by Burke but is concentrated against the individualism of the revolution, with which they assume Rousseau to be identified. The abstract individual, the man of the state of nature, they reject entirely; the social status alone is for them natural to man.[1] 'L'auteur du *Contrat social* . . . ', writes Bonald, 'ne vit que l'individu et dans Europe ne vit que Genève; il confondit dans l'homme la domination avec la liberté, dans la société la turbulence avec la force, . . . et il voulut réduire en théorie le gouvernement populaire, c'est-à-dire fixer l'inconstance et *ordonner* le désordre.'[2] Their fundamental argument is that on

[1] De Maistre, *Œuvres*, 1884-6, ii. 540-1, 548-9: *Examen d'un écrit de J.J. Rousseau*.

[2] Bonald, *Œuvres complètes*, 1859, i. 1091.

the basis of will, whether individual or general, no theory of sovereignty can be erected: the will of the people is just what can never be sovereign.[1] Agreeing with Rousseau that only the law can be sovereign, they disagreed with him because they held that the law can never be the result of human will, but only of divine ordinance. Starting from such a principle it was inevitable that the *Contrat social* should be for them, in the words of Lamennais before his recantation, 'a sacrilegious declaration of war against society and against God',[2] and this, in spite of certain merits that Bonald grants to Rousseau, sums up their attitude.

Whereas the theocrats, themselves maintaining in the name of Catholicism an extreme theory of authority, saw in Rousseau the protestant and the individualist, for constitutional or liberal political writers he was the teacher of the Jacobins and the upholder of the tyranny of the state. Of the criticism from this angle Benjamin Constant provides the best, as well as the best known, illustration. Practically every subsequent critic of Rousseau has quoted his indictment of the *Contrat social* as, 'le plus terrible auxiliaire de tous les genres de despotisme'. None take the trouble to cite the more detailed judgment in which he says, 'qu'en transportant dans nos temps modernes une étendue de pouvoir social, de souveraineté collective qui appartenait à d'autres siècles, ce génie sublime qu'animait l'amour le plus pur de la liberté a fourni néanmoins de funestes prétextes à plus d'un genre de tyrannie,' and adds, 'J'eviterai certès de me joindre aux détracteurs d'un grand homme.'[3] Elsewhere he turns his pen against these same detractors—'une tourbe d'esprits subalternes qui placent leur succès d'un jour à révoquer en doute toutes les vérités courageuses, s'agite pour flétrir sa gloire: raison de plus pour être circonspect à la blamer. Il a, le premier, rendu populaire le sentiment de nos droits. A sa voix, se sont réveillés les cœurs généreux, les âmes indépendantes; mais ce qu'il sentait avec force, il n'a pas su le définir avec précision.'[4]

Constant was still too near the revolution and too much influenced by the tradition of the early revolutionaries, to be able to forget that there had been a time when the author of the

[1] De Maistre, *Œuvres*, i. 465 : *Étude sur la souveraineté*.
[2] Lamennais, *Essai sur l'indifférence*, 1817, i. 280.
[3] B. Constant, *Cours de politique constitutionelle* (1818-20), 1861, ii. 549.
[4] B. Constant, *op. cit.*, i. 276 n.

Contrat social had been the idol of liberal France. In the next generation the criticism from this flank was more extreme. We may take as an example Lamartine, a more successful poet than politician, it is true, who nevertheless devoted a work to the refutation of Rousseau, whom he joins with Plato and Fénelon in a general condemnation. His point of view can be appreciated from what he has to say of Plato: 'Il ne manque au code du divin Platon que l'anthropophagie pour être la cloaque contre nature et contre humanité des immondices de la turpitude, de la démence et de la brutalité humaine.'[1] His verdict on Rousseau is longer but not substantially different.

The difficulty for most liberals in France, which prevented them from seeing that individualism in Rousseau which the theocrats had seen almost exclusively, was that they were brought up in the tradition of the *philosophes* and were therefore inevitably inheritors of the old enmity to the author of the *Vicaire Savoyard*. This applies without exception to the *idéologues*, and to the positivists who continued the tradition; particular illustrations are therefore hardly necessary.

The early socialists were more divided in opinion, and for them, of course, the individualism of Rousseau was his crime. According to some modern critics Rousseau's *Discours sur l'inégalité* should be regarded as one of the principal sources of the socialist movement of the next century, still more of anarchism. If this be so his followers were singularly ungrateful to their alleged master. With one or two exceptions, such as Louis Blanc, the Saint-Simonians and the early socialists were consistently hostile to Rousseau. Proudhon, in this if in no other respect typical, puts the grounds for enmity explicitly. 'C'est Rousseau qui nous apprend que le peuple, être collectif, n'a pas d'existence unitaire; que c'est une personne abstraite, une individualité morale, incapable par elle-même de penser, agir, se mouvoir.'[2] For him as for most of the socialists, the social contract was nothing but 'l'alliance offensive et défensive de ceux qui possèdent contre ceux que ne possèdent pas,' 'le code de la tyrannie capitaliste et mercantile.'[3]

In the earlier part of the century the sociologists and philo-

---

[1] Lamartine, *J.J. Rousseau. Son faux contrat social*, ed. of 1926, p. 19.
[2] P.-J. Proudhon, *Œuvres complètes*, 1923-36, ii. 193: *Idée générale de la Révolution au XIXᵉ siècle* (1851).
[3] *id.*, ii. 191, 194.

sophers were the chief enemies of Rousseau, while his adherents, in another order of ideas it is true, were to be found in the literary world, with writers such as George Sand. 'Quant à moi,' she wrote, when the current of ideas had changed, 'je lui reste fidèle. . . . Il m'a transmis comme à tous les artistes de mon temps, l'amour de la nature, l'enthousiasme du vrai, le mépris de la vie factice et le dégoût des vanités du monde.' [1] But French literature has always been characterized by an attachment to the opposition in politics, and when the republic had triumphed a sentimental conservatism and a tone of condemnation towards the revolution and all its works came into fashion. The link between the earlier sociological criticism and the later literary attack on Rousseau is provided by Taine, a writer whose hostility to Rousseau, as to the revolution, is all the more marked because it combines both motives of opposition. As he is free from the prejudices of the *philosophes*, however, there is at the same time in Taine, though hardly in his successors, a more generous appreciation of what he regards as the better qualities of Rousseau—'homme étrange, original et supérieur, . . . ayant commis des extravagances, des vilenies et des crimes, et néanmoins gardant jusqu'au bout la sensibilité délicate et profonde, l'humanité, l'attendrissement, le don des larmes, la faculté d'aimer, la passion de la justice, le sentiment religieux, l'enthousiasme, comme autant de racines vivaces où fermente toujours la sève généreuse pendant que la tige et les rameaux avortent, se déforment, ou se flétrissent sous l'inclémence de l'air.' [2] Even so qualified, praise from such an enemy as Taine is worth recording. But in drawing the picture of Rousseau's politics Taine leaves no half shades. 'A la souveraineté du roi, le *Contrat social* substitue la souveraineté du peuple. Mais la seconde est encore plus absolue que la première, et, dans le couvent démocratique que Rousseau construit sur le modèle de Sparte et de Rome, l'individu n'est rien, l'Etat est tout.' [3]

From Taine practically all the modern literary criticism of Rousseau is derived, and it cannot be said to add much to his arguments. With Brunetière it becomes more acute, and with later critics inconceivably shrill and bitter. To a certain extent

[1] 'A propos des Charmettes', *Revue des Deux Mondes*, 1863, vol. 48, pp. 341-65.
[2] H. Taine, *L'ancien régime*, 1876, pp. 289-90.
[3] H. Taine, *op. cit.*, p. 321.

this is because the religious motive was reintroduced to reinforce the political; but the hostility to Rousseau derived perhaps its most violent feelings from literary sources. In the periodic attempts to overthrow the prestige of the great writers of the romantic period in the interests of supposed classical principles, Rousseau has always been the chief enemy, and rightly, for his literary conquests are among the greatest, the most vulnerable and the most triumphantly inexpugnable of all the achievements of French romanticism. He represents, wrote Texte, the breach with all the traditions of French classical literature,[1] and above all French literature of the seventeenth and eighteenth centuries in which the classical virtues were supposed to be exemplified. Rousseau is not only alien to the classical literary tradition, he is hardly even French. That there was a chasm between the French eighteenth-century mind and his own he admitted. 'Je ne connais pas deux Français qui pussent parvenir à me connaître, quand même ils le désireraient de tout leur cœur,' he wrote.[2] And this intellectual cleavage is perhaps in itself partly responsible for the constant and envenomed hostility to a genius felt to be different, and therefore dangerous.

Because Rousseau was denounced by those who saw him as the prophet of the totalitarian state, it must not be supposed that he won the applause of those who went to the other extreme in giving the state priority over the individual. Rousseau's name is often associated with the German Idealists and he is not infrequently credited with being the real originator of their political system. Thus Duguit, summing up as wide an accusation as possible in one sentence, declares, 'J.-J. Rousseau est le père du despotisme jacobin, de la dictature césarienne, et à y regarder de près l'inspirateur des doctrines absolutistes de Kant et de Hegel.'[3]

The association of the strict Hegelian theory if not with absolute government at least with the magnification of the power of the state can hardly be doubted, and if we are to attribute this to the influence of Rousseau it cannot but affect our interpretation

[1] J. Texte, Rousseau et les origines du cosmopolitisme littéraire, 1885, p. 404.

[2] Œuvres (ed. of 1826, Badouin Frères), xviii. 317 n. Rousseau juge de Jean-Jacques, Second Dialogue.

[3] Duguit, op. cit., p. 6.

of his ideas. Without embarking on the question of his influence, we can appropriately ask what the Idealists themselves said of him and if they proclaimed their allegiance to his ideas. To begin with, the filiation between the thought of Rousseau and that of Kant is self-evident. The philosopher of the Pure Reason speaks in the highest terms of the writer from whom he had learnt to recognize the limits of the intellect as the Enlightenment had conceived it, and the importance of immediate sensation. It was Rousseau, he said, who had taught him to honour men. Rousseau, too, certainly contributed to his development of the principle of the autonomy of the will, by means of which he reconciled law with liberty. Kant's praise of Rousseau, however, belongs to the eighteenth-century current of thought, as does the early admiration of Fichte and Hegel. In 1793 Fichte was writing of Rousseau as one who had aroused the human mind to a consciousness of all its powers. But in Fichte we can see at work the process which led from the liberalism of the early revolutionary period, through the nationalism of the struggle against Napoleon, to the political philosophy of Hegel and the idealist state. Hegel, also, though he began with admiration for Rousseau, as his theory of the state evolved developed into a severe critic. There was too much of the individualist, the disciple of Locke, the upholder of individual rights in Rousseau to satisfy him.

One of the more recent onslaughts on Rousseau is that of Professor Talmon, according to whom Rousseau's general will was the driving force behind the rise of totalitarian democracy.[1] Talmon supports his case first on an analysis of Rousseau's 'totalitarian Messianic temperament'. In Rousseau, he says, 'the disciplinarian was the envious dream of the tormented paranoiac'.[2] This is the familiar method of Taine and many another French literary critic from the right, who on the basis of the ideas he is supposed to have held deduce the character of a writer, and then in turn justify their interpretation of his ideas on the basis of his supposed character. It is surprising that Professor Talmon should resort to this method, for he recognizes elsewhere clearly enough what the general will is for Rousseau.

---

[1] J. L. Talmon, *The Origins of Totalitarian Democracy*, 1952, p. 6.
[2] *id.*, p. 39.

It is, in the last resort, he says, a Cartesian truth,[1] 'something like a mathematical truth or a Platonic idea',[2] and 'ultimately a question of enlightenment and morality'.[3] This is perceptive. The application of such ideas to politics undoubtedly brings dangers with it, but whatever Professor Popper may have said in his *Open Society and its Enemies*—again with much truth mixed with fundamental historical distortions—these ideas are not to be reasonably dismissed as mere paranoiac illusions. And when Professor Talmon tries to show that totalitarianism is what the general will meant for Rousseau, he can only do so by ignoring all Rousseau's practical qualifications of his theoretical discussion and even changing the sense of what he says.

It is suggested, for example, that the general will implies unanimity, and that this has to be engineered by such methods as intimidation and electoral trickery.[4] Undoubtedly these were the methods of totalitarian democracy, but the point is irrelevant since of course Rousseau's general will does not imply unanimity. Again, we are told that 'there is nothing that Rousseau insists on more than the active and ceaseless participation of the people and of every citizen in the affairs of the state'.[5] In fact, what the people must participate in is the law-making process, and this, according to him, is a rare and exceptional activity; from the executive acts of government the sovereign people is rigorously excluded. We are told that Rousseau's thought passes into a collectivism of an organic and historical type.[6] Apart from the fact that these are quite different types of collectivism, M. Derathé has shown how mistaken it is to identify Rousseau's thought with either. Finally, it is suggested that Rousseau puts the people in place of the Physiocratic absolute sovereign.[7] It is interesting to find that, long before Professor Talmon wrote, but after the first edition of this book appeared, a French writer devoted a whole work to demonstrating precisely the opposite. 'A Quesnay,' this critic writes, 'il faut opposer Jean-Jacques

[1] *id.*, p. 29.
[2] *id.*, p. 41.
[3] *id.*, p. 42.
[4] *id.*, p. 46.
[5] *id.*, p. 47.
[6] *id.*, p. 280.
[7] *id.*, p. 46.

Rousseau et au mythe de l'ordre naturel le civisme'.[1] Rousseau does indeed put his finger on the weak spot of physiocratic theory: 'On commence par rechercher les règles dont, pour l'utilité commune, il serait à propos que les hommes convinssent entre eux; et puis on donne le nom de *loi naturelle* à la collection de ces règles, sans autre preuve que le bien qu'on trouve qui résulterait de leur pratique universelle. Voilà assurément une manière très commode de composer des définitions et d'expliquer la nature des choses par des convenances presque arbitraires.[2] Rousseau's criticism is one which can be applied not only to the Physiocrats but to Saint-Simon, Fourier, Marx—in fact, to the creators of any great historical philosophy.[3] There is more excuse for linking him with the German philosophers, as does Cassirer, according to whom Kant was the only man in the eighteenth century to understand the inner cohesion of Rousseau's thought.[4] Rousseau, says Cassirer, subordinated politics to the ethical imperative, and was not interested in happiness or utility.[5] This seems to me to go much too far, but at least it recognises the essential ethical quality of Rousseau's thought.

It is not my purpose in this chapter to examine the value of the multifarious and mutually contradictory verdicts that have been passed on the political thought of Rousseau, but merely to indicate their variety, and the constancy with which they fall into one or other of the two chief categories—Rousseau the individualist, Rousseau the prophet of state absolutism—neither of which seems a satisfactory interpretation of his whole thought. It may be that no synthesis of his ideas is possible, that they have to be put into one or other of two contradictory groups, but on the other hand the confusion may have arisen partly from reading back into Rousseau his supposed historical influence, partly from an attempt to force his thought into theoretical categories that he never had in mind when he wrote.

---

[1] Ch. Bourthoumieux, *Essai sur le fondement philosophique des doctrines économiques. Rousseau contre Quesnay*, 1936, p. 134. A direct criticism of Professor Talmon's interpretation of Rousseau is John W. Chapman's *Rousseau —Totalitarian or Liberal?*, 1956.

[2] *Pol. Writings*, i. 137: *Discours sur l'inégalité*, p. 170.

[3] Bourthoumieux, p. 124.

[4] E. Cassirer, *The Question of Jean-Jacques Rousseau*, translated and edited by Peter Gay, 1954, pp. 21, 70.

[5] *id.*, pp. 66, 71.

CHAPTER II

THE POLITICAL WORLD OF ROUSSEAU

1. PHILOSOPHES AND DESPOTS

It is not always remembered that a general statement about the power of the state tells us practically nothing unless we know what are the conditions laid down for its exercise, and above all of what kind of state we are talking at any particular time. In some schools of political writing the latter is a question to which we never find the answer, because what is said of one state is assumed to be automatically true of all states, as though the state were a natural species of which certain qualities can necessarily be predicated, instead of being an artificial construction of almost endless variety in its forms. Rousseau, however, distinguishes between the various states of his own day and of the past, discusses sometimes the possibly improved state into which they might be developed by a wise legislator, and sometimes his ideal state, which he has practically no hope of seeing realized in the world of hard facts. For the purposes of our discussion we have also to bear in mind yet another type of state, that, namely, which has developed since his day, and which differs in many essential respects from the state of the eighteenth century. I propose to consider first Rousseau's judgment on the state as it was in his own time, reserving for subsequent consideration his theory of the ideal state, his tendencies as a practical reformer, and the possible application of his ideas to the type of state that has since evolved.

Taking in the first place the eighteenth-century state, it must be said that so far as this is concerned he is clearly not an adherent of the theory of absolute state authority. When we read his comments on the despotisms that he saw around him we cannot but ask whether the reaction against revolutionary enthusiasm has gone far enough and perhaps too far, whether the earlier view that took Rousseau as one of the founders of 'liberal Europe' and a firm enemy of despotism is not after all the truer starting-point for a study of his thought.

Roughly, French political thought in the latter half of the eighteenth century can be divided into two schools—the one formed by the followers of Montesquieu, the other by the rest. Practically all the constitutional ideas of the century in France go back to Montesquieu. A hatred of despotic government runs like a bright thread through the complicated tapestry of his writings and outlines the pattern of his thought. His disciples are indicated by their belief in moderate constitutional government, in the separation of powers and in the rule of law, but few of the leading thinkers of the century are to be found in this group. The first generation of physiocrats believed in despotism, even if it were that kind of 'legal despotism' which they said, rather optimistically, 'n'est autre chose que la force naturelle et irrésistible de l'évidence'.[1] Most of the *philosophes* gave expression to more liberal views, but they accepted favours from Frederick or Catherine, or such of the lesser despots as could afford to take up the fashionable role of patronizing philosophy, and in France itself, while to a certain extent they undermined the position of the *noblesse*, they breathed scarcely a word of criticism on the monarchy.

Diderot is an exception to this statement, for the most violent attacks on despots are to be found in his writings, together with an unqualified proclamation of the legislative sovereignty of the people. Though his hostility to kings was not wholly proof against the flattery of an Empress, in the *Mémoirs* he drew up for Catherine he maintained with unexpected force his advanced political principles, and condemned even enlightened despotism.[2] It is said that Raynal owed the extremer passages in his *Histoire des Deux Indes* to Diderot, and subsequently disavowed them.

Voltaire represents a more difficult case. He supported the rule of law and was the untiring advocate of personal liberties. In *Idées républicaines*, although his intention has been questioned, he probably was sincerely writing in the interests of the more democratic party in Geneva.[3] Such sentiments as 'la liberté consiste à ne dépendre que des lois',[4] or 'je vous avouerai que je

---

[1] H. Sée, *L'Évolution de la pensée politique en France au XVIIIe siècle*, 1925, p. 210: quoted from *Lemercier de la Rivière*.

[2] M. Tourneux, *Diderot et Catherine II*, 1899, p. 143.

[3] cf. Peter Gay, *Voltaire's Politics*, 1959, pp. 214-18.

[4] Voltaire, *Œuvres*, 1877-85, xviii. 526: *Pensées sur le Gouvernement*, 1752.

C

m'accorderais assez d'un gouvernement démocratique',[1] and his admiration for the liberty he discovered in England, seem genuine enough. In France, on the other hand, he was an upholder of the *thèse royale*. His connections with Frederick and Catherine are far from showing Voltaire at his best. The danger of a generous and even liberal outlook on society without the safeguard of political principles is exhibited in Voltaire's practical judgments. As Professor Gay, who justly defends Voltaire from the more severe condemnation of his critics, rightly says, 'He never achieved Rousseau's insight that a stratified absolutism like Frederick's, which offered the middle classes no political education, was an authoritarian defence against constitutionalism and civil liberties, rather than a transitional step toward them'.[2]

Mably is nearer to Rousseau in many of his political ideas, but most of the *philosophes* inclined politically in the direction of the *status quo*. Their end, it has been said, was not liberty but efficiency; and in this they look forward to the Napoleonic despotism, and the omni-competent state of the nineteenth century.

Rousseau, on the other hand, as the greatest of the disciples of Montesquieu,[3] is a consistent critic of the benevolent despots and as clear an upholder of the rule of law as Locke himself. If timidity prevented him from making definite attacks on existing governments, which moreover he avoided on principle, in a letter he admits his dislike for kings and says that he is no friend to monarchical government, although he has followed the custom of the gypsies, he adds, in always sparing in their incursions the house that sheltered them.[4] But we must not look to him for praise of kings. Even Milord Maréchal's king, and Rousseau's protector in Neuchâtel, won little approval from him, a favourable letter of 1766 representing no more than politeness and gratitude.[5] Earlier he told a correspondent that however much he admired the ability of the king of Prussia he was not to be counted among his partisans. 'Je ne puis estimer ni aimer un

---

[1] *id.*, xxvii. 347: *L'A.B.C.*, 1768.

[2] Gay, p. 170.

[3] *cf.* E. Carcassonne, *Montesquieu et le problème de la constitution française au XVIIIᵉ siècle*, s.d., pp. 325-32.

[4] *Corr. Gén.*, viii. 68: to Milord Maréchal, August 1762.

[5] *id.*, xv. 133: to the King of Prussia, March 30, 1766.

homme sans principes, qui foule aux pieds tout droit des gens.'[1] It is curious that the integrity of a writer whose austere political principles saved him from the relation of royal patron and literary eulogist should be compared unfavourably with that of the flatterers, however insincere, of the benevolent despots. Consider, for instance, Rousseau's constant rejection of offers of patronage from Russia, and compare with it such a letter as that from Voltaire to Mme du Deffand in which he prides himself on being in Catherine's favour and refers as a mere bagatelle to the little affair of the murder of her husband.[2] Rousseau could indeed afford to write to Voltaire, not without pride, that he had rightly judged him a republican, and one who adored liberty and detested domination and servitude.[3] It is true that nowhere subsequently does he speak quite so frankly of despotism as in the Discours sur l'inégalité; but his letter to Mirabeau of 1767 serves to show that his enmity was unwavering. 'Ne me parlez plus de votre despotisme légal. Je ne saurais le goûter, ni même l'entendre; et je ne vois là que deux mots contradictoires.'[4]

It is remarkable that no attempt was made to suppress the Discours sur l'inégalité, a profoundly revolutionary work. This essay strikes the keynote when it speaks of 'le despotisme, élevant par degrés sa tête hideuse'; and the note is repeated many times.[5] Two evils Rousseau particularly singles out as characteristic of the despotic system; first, that it means government by favourites, with all the accompanying inefficiency and corruption.[6] The second and fundamental one is the to him atrocious possibility that in the state any individual or party can be above the law. Reiterated time and again in his writings, it is the almost exclusive theme of the Lettres de la Montagne. The basis of his protest against the Genevan authorities was that they were attempting to override the law of the state and to set their will above the decrees of the sovereign legislative body. 'La pire des lois,' he cries, 'vaut encore mieux que le meilleur maître.'[7] 'Un

[1] id., iv. 149-50: October 4, 1758.
[2] Œuvres, xlv. 267-8 (May 18, 1767).
[3] Corr. Gén., i. 302: January 30, 1750.
[4] Pol. Writings, ii. 161.
[5] e.g. id., i. 193-4, 314; ii. 161.
[6] id., i. 418; ii. 78, 80, 511.
[7] id., ii. 235: Lett. Mont., viii.

peuple est libre' — his words might be quoted from Burke —
'quelque forme qu'ait son Gouvernement, quand, dans celui qui
le gouverne, il ne voit point l'homme, mais l'organe de la Loi.'[1]

Where there is a ruler above the law, for Rousseau not merely
is the people not free—as a people, as an organized state, it does
not exist at all. In the person of an absolute ruler he sees force
incarnate, disguised internally under the title of law, and exter-
nally under that of *raison d'état*.[2] Despotism is merely a
synonym for the rule of force, and the despot is only the master
so long as he is the strongest.[3] When the only power holding the
people together is the will of the ruler, as soon as the tyrant
ceases to be the most powerful, the state disintegrates into its
constituent fragments.[4] With this we arrive at Rousseau's fundamental objection to absolute monarchy as a form of government.
Under it, he holds, the state is a mere collection of individuals, in
no way a community, at best a sort of conscript army and at
worst a rabble.

The logical consequence of Rousseau's denunciation of despotic
government is revolution, as he himself recognized in the
Discours sur l'inégalité, where he wrote that since the rights of
government depended on the fundamental laws, if these were
destroyed the magistrates ceased to be legitimate and the people
were no longer bound to obey them. Since not the magistrate
but the law constituted the essence of the state, each individual
would thus recover his natural liberty. And he concluded,
'L'émeute qui finit par étrangler ou détrôner un sultan est un
acte aussi juridique que ceux par lesquels il disposait la veille des
vies et des biens de ses sujets. La seule force le maintenait, la seule
force le renverse.'[5] Mercier, who complained that Rousseau did
not mention insurrection as a legitimate recourse of an oppressed
people,[6] was in fact mistaken, for such was the nemesis which,
whether he desired it or not, Rousseau certainly foretold on the
despotic governments of the *ancien régime*. However much he

---

[1] *loc. cit*.; cf. *id*., i. 126; ii. 204, 208-9.
[2] *id*., i. 304: *L'état de guerre*.
[3] *id*., i. 194: *Disc. inég*.
[4] *id*., i. 468: *Con. soc*. (first version).
[5] *id*., i. 188, 194.
[6] L.-S. Mercier, *De J.-J. Rousseau considéré comme l'un des premiers Auteurs
de la Révolution*, 1791, i. 60.

may proclaim his antipathy to revolution, the fact cannot be concealed that consciously or unconsciously, in drawing up the plan of an ideal state he was inevitably proposing a revolutionary end: as Beaulavon puts it, to determine the conditions of a just state is to point out the road to those who love justice.[1]

Nor was the revolutionary strain in his writings merely latent. Vaughan argues from the character of the earlier chapters of the *Contrat social* that Rousseau when he wrote them was prepared to see the contract introduced by revolutionary means,[2] and indeed the interpretation of some of his phrases is hardly ambiguous. We cannot misconceive his meaning when he writes, 'Ce n'est pas que, comme quelques maladies bouleversent la tête des hommes et leur ôtent le souvenir du passé, il ne se trouve quelquefois dans la durée des Etats des époques violentes où les révolutions font sur les peuples ce que certaines crises font sur les individus: où l'horreur du passé tient lieu d'oubli, et où l'Etat, embrasé par les guerres civiles, renaît pour ainsi dire de sa cendre, et reprend la vigueur de la jeunesse en sortant des bras de la mort'.[3] He goes beyond the theoretic justification of revolution to prophesies of its inevitability and its imminence. In the *Emile* he says, 'Nous approchons de l'état de crise et du siècle des révolutions'.[4] Again, 'Je vois tous les Etats de l'Europe courir à leur ruine',[5] while the famous letter to Milord Maréchal, which chanced to be written in 1768, declares, 'Si la nation française est avilie, c'est par le fait d'autrui, et non par le sien propre. Souvenez-vous, milord, qu'elle ne sera pas vile dans vingt ans.'[6]

It is true, of course, that Rousseau's language does not necessarily imply violent change; indeed Mercier represents him as saying in 1775 that there would be no civil war in France: the blind folly of the court on the one hand, the excessive abuses and increasing enlightment on the other, would prevent any effective resistance.[7] And of course, when we come to questions of actual

---

[1] Beaulavon, *op. cit.*, p. 17.

[2] *Pol. Writings*, i. 439.

[3] *id.*, ii. 55: *Con. soc.*, II. viii.

[4] *Œuvres*, iii. 327: *Émile*, III. He adds in a note, 'J'ai de mon opinion des raisons plus particulières que cette maxime; mais il n'est pas à propos de les dire, et chacun ne les voit que trop'.

[5] *Pol. Writings*, ii. 425: *Gouv. Pol.*

[6] *id.*, ii. 16 n.

[7] Mercier, *op. cit.*, ii. 210-11 n.

politics we find that Rousseau is timidity incarnate. In his *Rousseau juge de Jean-Jacques* he complained that his enemies had represented him as a sedition monger, and treated his love of constitutional liberty as an appeal to frantic licence.[1] His apparent fear of revolution is not to be taken, as Vaughan suggests, merely as a development of the later years of his life. In the dedication to his most revolutionary work, the *Discours sur l'inégalité*, is to be found a warning against revolution that, as one cannot help remarking more than a few times in reading Rousseau, might have come from the pen of Burke. 'Les peuples une fois accoutumés à des maîtres ne sont plus en état de s'en passer. S'ils tentent de secouer le joug, ils s'éloignent d'autant plus de la liberté, que, prenant pour elle une licence effrénée qui lui est opposée, leurs révolutions les livrent presque toujours à des séducteurs qui ne font qu'aggraver leurs chaînes.'[2] His *Réponse au Roi de Pologne* of 1752 expresses the opinion that a great revolution is almost as much to be feared as the evils it might be intended to remedy, and that in any case such a revolution should not be desired and cannot be foreseen.[3] His *Jugement sur la Polysynodie* is equally severe against revolutionary changes, especially in such a great country as France. What intelligent man, he asks, would dare to propose to abolish the old customs, to change the ancient principles, and to give the state any other form than that which has been produced by thirteen centuries of history.[4] As for the *Lettres de la Montagne*, their frequent invocations against civil disturbance, and injunctions that even liberty is too dearly bought at the price of bloodshed, are well known.[5] The same advice is repeated in his correspondence about Geneva with d'Ivernois. 'La paix, mes amis,' he counsels, 'la paix, et promptement, ou je meurs de peur que tout n'aille mal.'[6] The solution he counsels is based on the acceptance of a compromise and the recognition of the legitimate authority of the magistrates of the city. In republics, he says, respect for the magistrates constitutes the glory of the city.[7]

[1] *Œuvres*, xi. 318: *Rousseau juge de Jean-Jacques, Second Dialogue.*
[2] *Pol. Writings*, i. 127.
[3] *id.*, i. 439, n. 2.
[4] *id.*, i. 416.
[5] *cf. id.*, ii. 229, 244-5, n. 4, 246.
[6] *Corr. Gén.*, xviii. 135: to d'Ivernois, February 23, 1768; *cf. id.*, pp. 82, 99, 115.
[7] *id.*, xviii. 176: to d'Ivernois, March 24, 1768.

Rousseau is moreover in constant fear of seeming to criticise the actual government of France. For it is of France particularly that he is thinking when he writes, for instance, 'J'eus et j'aurai toujours pour maxime inviolable de porter le plus profond respect au Gouvernement sous lequel je vis, sans me mêler de vouloir jamais le censurer et critiquer, ou réformer en aucune manière'.[1] To put an end to these citations, it is difficult if not impossible, as Mercier is compelled to confess, to find in Rousseau, despite his theoretical hostility to despotism, anything positive concerning a right to change an established government by force.[2] In the end, then, if we confine ourselves to the political sphere we find that Rousseau, though with some hesituation, comes down definitely on the moderate side and against revolution. An examination of his works cannot but confirm the conclusions of Mornet who, writing that in political matters neither Voltaire, nor Montesquieu, nor Diderot were revolutionaries, perforce includes Rousseau in the same judgment,[3] in spite of which his condemnation of despotic government remains unqualified.

2. PARLIAMENTARY GOVERNMENT

Rousseau's hostility to the despotic governments of his day does not by itself justify the assumption that he favoured political liberty. It is still necessary to enquire what form his conception of political freedom takes, and above all whether for constitutional liberty he reads, as his critics allege, despotic democracy. His repeated criticisms of the English constitution seem to stand in the way of the more liberal interpretation, for it is generally taken for granted that England was as a matter of course to be regarded in the eighteenth century as the home of political freedom and the model of constitutional progress. England was still the land of Cromwell, Sidney and Locke, even though revolution had degenerated into riot and democracy seemed farther off even than in the days of Lilburne and Harrington.

Montesquieu himself, in his *Notes sur l'Angleterre*, had shown that he was not unaware of the grosser features of Whig

[1] *Corr. Gén.*, xiii. 151 : to Buttafoco, March 24, 1765.

[2] Mercier, *op. cit.*, ii. 3.

[3] D. Mornet, *Origines intellectuelles de la Révolution française, 1715-87*, 1933, p. 476.

political machinery, though in the *Esprit des Lois* he suppressed all mention of them. There was in fact always a strain of unfavourable criticism of the English constitution in France, which increased as the century went on, until by the time of the revolution the note of hostility was dominant. This evolution did not occur, as Janet and Dedieu held, about 1760, but some twenty years later, at the time of the American War. It can be attributed in part to a transference of admiration to the virile and romantic young republic of the West, and in part to an increased knowledge of the defects of the English parliamentary system.[1] D'Holbach's description sums up admirably the general verdict of France in the pre-revolutionary phase on the English constitution. The members of the House of Commons, once elected, he said, are no longer responsible to their electors, but much more dependent on the Court, to which they sacrifice the interests of their constituents.[2] By 1789 England was seen as the home not of freedom but of corruption. The English example was frequently quoted during the revolution, it is true, but generally against the constitutional parties. To give a single illustration, in England, writes Billaud-Varennes, 'L'intérêt de la nation est constamment sacrifié à l'ambition du souverain, . . . le grand art du ministère est de tenir dans son portefeuille le tarif des consciences'.[3] Not only the prevalent corruption, but also the unrepresentative character of the House of Commons, was well recognized in France. Another revolutionary critic, in an oration at the Jacobin Club, demanded, 'Peuple anglais, comment, parmi toi, se fait-il que ce soit le sol, le terrain, ou ce qu'on appelle propriété qui soit représenté dans la Chambre des Communes? Quoi! Les richesses seules ont le droit à gouverner?'[4]

It should be remembered that the dominant influence in the formation of eighteenth-century political ideas was classical; and when we turn to Rousseau the example of Calvinist Geneva was added to that of the ancient city state to establish a mode of political thinking markedly different from the English tradition. That Rousseau should be numbered among the critics of the

[1] G. Bonno, *La Constitution britannique devant l'opinion française de Montesquieu à Bonaparte*, 1932, pp. 273-5.

[2] d'Holbach, *Système social*, 1774, ii. 70-1.

[3] Billaud-Varennes, *L'Acéphocratie*, 1791, pp. 4-5.

[4] F. Lepelletier, in *Le Moniteur*, no. 137, February 5, 1794.

English system of government is, given all these circumstances, not surprising. At the same time it is not correct that in Rousseau the whole principles and practice of the English parliamentary monarchy are joined in a peremptory and summary condemnation.[1] What is really remarkable in fact is the moderation of his criticism, which left scope for an appreciation of what seemed to him the admirable features of the constitution, so that his disciple, Mercier, felt constrained to confess, 'En général Rousseau (on doit l'avouer) avait pour point de vue éternel la Suisse sa patrie et un peu l'Angleterre'.[2] The two—Geneva and England—are closely associated in the Lettres de la Montagne, where his defence of the constitutional liberties of Geneva is supported by citation of the example of England, which provides, he says, a model of the just balance of powers, where the law, leaving the king no power to do mischief, leaves him a great power to do good.[3] The eulogy of English political institutions in the Nouvelle Héloïse, placed appropriately in a letter from my lord Edouard, is well known. 'Passé chez la seule nation d'hommes qui reste parmi les troupeaux divers dont la terre est couverte, si vous n'avez pas vu régner les loix, vous les avez vu du moins exister encore; vous avez appris à quels signes on reconnaît cet organe sacré de la volonté d'un peuple, et comment l'empire de la raison publique est le vrai fondement de la liberté.'[4]

Rousseau's attack on the English constitution can be reduced to a criticism of one particular feature, to which he is opposed on general theoretic grounds, the system of representation. One explanation that has been proffered for Rousseau's persistent hostility to this is his opposition to the Petit Conseil at Geneva, which claimed the right of acting as the representative of the people.[5] There is no more than a verbal connection here, however, for the claim of the Petit Conseil was not based on any actual system of representation, and Rousseau's attitude is to be attributed to more fundamental considerations. In his criticism of the functioning of the English representative system, what Rousseau opposes is not the inadequacy of the English electoral

---

[1] Bonno, op. cit., pp. 33-4.
[2] Mercier, op. cit., ii. 5 n.
[3] Pol. Writings, ii. 266, 271.
[4] La Nouvelle Héloïse, ed. Mornet, 1925, iv. 2.
[5] G. Vallette, Jean-Jacques Rousseau genevoise, 1911, pp. 190-1.

rolls. This fact, even had he been aware of it, would not necessarily have appeared to him as a defect: the citizenship of Geneva was itself narrowly restricted, but he never raised his voice on behalf of his unenfranchised fellow-townsmen. So, in England his criticism is directed almost exclusively against the English parliament's peculiar independence of its constituents, whence arises his famous saying that the English people is only free during the election of members of parliament.[1] He comments on the undue length of time elapsing between elections, which enables members to become almost entirely independent of their constituents, and as a natural consequence to fall under the influence of royal corruption.[2] As a result of this, within twenty years, he believes, the English will have shared the fate of the Danes and the Swiss and will have lost their liberty, or rather, as he corrects himself elsewhere, the relics of their liberty.[3] Such is his interpretation of the Middlesex election controversy. Admitting that Wilkes stood for nothing in himself, nevertheless by the example of his exclusion a precedent had been established, and henceforth only those members who were agreeable to the Court would be allowed to take their seats in the Commons.[4] It is easy to see that Rousseau is taking Whig denunciations of royal interference at their face value, though his comments are not without shrewdness.

From all this we may conclude that Rousseau's observations on the English political system are not to be taken as evidence of a general dislike of constitutional government, still less of any hankering after a despotic system. He never denied that the government of England was a free one as compared with those prevailing in most other countries. Corruption, he allowed, if an abuse of liberty, is also a proof that liberty exists. 'Tout Anglais, à l'abris des lois, peut braver la puissance royale.'[5] Nor, again, was the criticism by Rousseau of much importance in causing the decline of admiration for the English constitution in France.[6] In the *Gouvernement de Pologne* he even relaxes his ban against representation, which he is now willing to accept, so long as

---

[1] *Pol. Writings*, ii. 96: *Con. soc.*, III. xv.
[2] *id.*, ii. 448, 450: *Gouv. Pol.*
[3] *id.*, i. 373, n. 1; ii. 464; *Corr. Gén.*, v. 300.
[4] *id.*, ii. 454: *Gouv. Pol.*
[5] *id.*, ii. 266, 267, 271: *Lett. Mont.*, IX.
[6] Bonno, *op. cit.*, p. 35.

there are frequent diets and the representatives are strictly compelled to follow the instructions of their constituents; they are left free, moreover, to decide for themselves any unanticipated question which may arise.[1] Nevertheless, whatever modifications he may introduce later, it is not a false notion which has led some commentators to fix on this question of representation and his consequent criticism of the English constitution as one of the vital points in Rousseau's political thought. On his principles the representative would be reduced, one must admit, to a mere delegate, bound hand and foot by instructions, limited by referendum and recall, and at best only allowed to exercise what functions remained to him for a very limited period. It is only fair to add that his authority was purely legislative: to have proposed such restrictions on an executive agent would have been ridiculous and Rousseau made no such attempt.

To do full justice to Rousseau it is necessary to remember that in the eighteenth century the modern representative system existed only in embryo, and that the medieval idea of representation, which still survived, did not necessarily imply election. To put it crudely, a great landowner might in a sense be considered to represent his land, and therefore the communities on it. Representation, of course, was always of communities, not of individuals—but this is perhaps not such a mistaken idea, for it might be held that a community, or at least its ideals and interests, can be represented, whereas an individual cannot. The idea of representation as a quality especially inherent in the landed aristocracy is particularly evident in Burke's theory of 'virtual representation'. This assumed the existence of a privileged, hereditary governing class, and at bottom was the very conception against which Rousseau was revolting. The attempt to concentrate an hereditary authority in the hands of a certain number of families was, he held, the greatest abuse in Genevan political life.[2] That Rousseau envisaged representation in the older sense is shown in the *Contrat social*, where in so many words he points out the medieval origin of the principle.[3] He was

---

[1] *Pol. Writings*, ii. 450-2: *Gouv. Pol.*, VII.

[2] *Corr. Gén.*, xviii. 15: to d'Ivernois, February 9, 1768.

[3] *Pol. Writings*, ii. 96: *Con. soc.*, III. xv. 'L'idée des Représentants est moderne [i.e. not classical]: elle nous vient du Gouvernement féodal, de cet inique et absurde Gouvernement dans lequel l'éspèce humaine est dégradée, et où le nom d'homme est en déshonneur.'

still sufficiently a man of his century for this to be in itself a ground for condemnation.

On this, as on many other points, what he says is, as he himself claims, implicit in Locke, and all that he is doing is to draw the obvious practical conclusions.[1] But when Locke had been read existing political conditions had been taken for granted. His arguments had been utilized against the Stuart monarchy and it had hardly been seen what dangerous implications they contained for the whole aristocratic political system. Rousseau, however, had no desire to see the power of the despotic monarchy abolished to the advantage of the privileged classes. So long as the old idea of representation, exemplified in the English constitution and in the claims of the oligarchy at Geneva, was present to his mind, it was natural that he should be an opponent of the representative system.

As a consequence of rejecting the principle of representation, Rousseau is compelled to confine the legislative power to the people, and if representatives are allowed, to treat them strictly as delegates. But without a clear recognition of what he understood by the sovereign people we will be liable to misinterpret his political creed. Nowhere does he allow the people in a political sense to be the whole adult, or even the whole adult male population. The *Lettres de la Montagne* is an appeal for moderate constitutional government, and an indictment of the attempt by a small oligarchy of ruling families to usurp the government of Geneva, but it is lacking in any plea for an extension of citizenship in a democratic direction. Yet the *Lettres de la Montagne* have been described as the *Provinciales* of political democracy and religious liberalism.[2] In them, and even more in the constitution for Poland, we find plenty of evidence of Rousseau's political caution, and his respect for historical tradition.[3]

From a modern point of view his conservatism may even seem excessive, since it does not permit him to contemplate the extension of political rights from the sixteen-hundred-odd citizens and bourgeois of Geneva to the many times more numerous, but always disenfranchised *habitants*, *natifs* and *sujets*. If one compares Rousseau's unquestioning acceptance of their political

---

[1] *id.*, ii. 206: *Lett. Mont.*, VI.

[2] G. Vallette, *op. cit.*, p. 295.

[3] As Vaughan points out, *e.g. Pol. Writings*, ii. 188.

inferiority with Locke's suggestions for the reform of the English franchise, the later thinker will not necessarily appear the more advanced.[1] It is not to make any new claim for political power on behalf of the populace of Geneva that Rousseau intervenes in the political controversy: it is of the sixteen hundred of the Conseil Général that he says, 'Il est la Loi vivante et fondamentale, qui donne vie et force à tout le reste, et qui ne connaît d'autres droits que les siens. Le Conseil général n'est pas un ordre dans l'Etat; il est l'Etat même.'[2]

In the sphere of practical politics Rousseau consistently favours what the eighteenth century called *gouvernement mixte*, formed by a balance of councils combining both the aristocratic and the democratic principles, 'où le peuple soit libre sans être maître et où le Magistrat commande sans tiranniser'.[3] But if there is nothing here in favour of a democratic franchise, equally there is nowhere the slightest willingness to accept despotic government. In spite of his opposition to the representative system, so far as concerns the governments of the eighteenth century and his own practical proposals for their amendment Rousseau is unmistakably on the side of moderate constitutional government. And if in the end he has to choose between the abuse of liberty and the abuse of power it is the former evil that he prefers, for 'l'abus de la liberté tourne au préjudice du peuple qui en abuse, et, le punissant de son propre tort, le force à en chercher le remède. Ainsi, de ce côté, le mal n'est jamais qu'une crise, il ne peut faire un état permanent; au lieu que l'abus de la puissance, ne tournant point au préjudice du puissant, mais du faible, est, par sa nature, sans mesure, sans frein, sans limites.'[4]

3. ASSOCIATIONS IN THE STATE

The real argument of those who believe Rousseau to have been an adherent of the absolutism of the state is provided not by any of the writings in which he applied his political principles to actually existing states but by his one theoretical treatise on

[1] Locke, *Second Discourse on Government*, §§ 157, 158.
[2] *Pol. Writings*, ii. 217: *Lett. Mont.*, IX.
[3] *Corr. Gén.*, xviii. 101: to Coindet, February 9, 1768; *cf. id.*, pp. 109-10.
[4] *Pol. Writings*, ii. 284: *Lett. Mont.*, IX.

politics. The *Contrat social* demands particular attention, because it undoubtedly embodies the most important ideas contributed by Rousseau to the development of political thought. Two arguments in particular produced in the *Contrat social* lend considerable support to those who see in the work primarily an attempt to justify the absolute state. Such seems to be the natural interpretation of his remarks on the civil religion and his objection to the existence of any smaller associations within the state.

There can be no doubt, to take the latter point first, that subordinate corporations present, as Montesquieu saw, a powerful barrier to the tyranny of the state. But while rightly stressing this fact, the author of the *Esprit des Lois* hardly took into consideration the possibilities that they themselves present for corruption and tyranny. As Beaulavon points out, when Rousseau denounced particular associations in the state he was thinking of the *Parlements* of France, of the *Petit Conseil* at Geneva,[1] and—we may add—of the network of petty privileged groups which were in effect so many barriers to liberty in France. On this point he was at one with all the enlightened thinkers of his time. Many illustrations might be found of the protest against the tyranny of corporations. To take only one from Helvétius: 'L'esprit de corps nous envahit de toutes parts. Sous le nom de corps, c'est un pouvoir qu'on érige aux dépens de la grande société. C'est par des usurpations héréditaires que nous sommes gouvernés. Sous le nom de Français, il n'existe que des corporations d'individus et pas un citoyen qui mérite ce titre.'[2] Rousseau himself does not go quite so far in his condemnation of corporations. If he condemns them in one chapter of the *Contrat social*,[3] in another he acknowledges the utility of subordinate corporations in monarchies.[4] What concerns him is partly the danger that the power of an association may pervert the General Will. He hardly seems to expect the extreme course of prohibiting all subsidiary associations in the state to be possible, since he proposes an alternative—'Que s'il y

[1] Beauvalon, *op. cit.*, p. 48, n. 2.

[2] Letter of Helvétius to Saurin; see also letter to Montesquieu, pp. 316-17: quoted by Tchernoff, 'Montesquieu et J.-J. Rousseau', *Revue du droit public*, vols. 19, 20, 1903

[3] *Pol. Writings*, ii. 42-3: *Con. soc.*, II. iii.

[4] *id.*, ii. 78: *Con. soc.*, III. vi.

a des sociétés partielles, il en faut multiplier le nombre et en prévenir l'inégalité'.[1]

Vaughan's criticism that the effect of Rousseau's theory of associations is to isolate the individual in the state and leave, as Burke had said, only detached units in face of an absolute state, is hardly a fair interpretation of his thought as a whole. It is only partially justified even by what he says in the *Contrat social*, and it leaves out of consideration other works in which, more concerned with practicability and less with theoretical perfection, he profoundly modifies his opinion. A passage in the *Economie politique*, embodying his clearest statement on this issue, puts forward a surprisingly modern view of the state, which he admits here to be a body made up of a nexus of smaller associations. 'Toute société politique est composée d'autres sociétés plus petites de différentes espèces, dont chacune a ses intérêts et ses maximes. . . . Ce sont toutes ces associations tacites ou formelles qui modifient de tant de manières les apparences de la volonté publique par l'influence de la leur.'[2] It is interesting to observe that Rousseau does not base himself on the assumption of an essential difference in nature between the association and the state. For him they both have a purely voluntary and contractual origin, and each constitutes a moral personality with a corporate will of its own. For Rousseau, says one writer, the state is an association which differs from other associations only by its extent and inclusiveness: its origin is the same.[3]

This verdict is too sweeping; the one essential distinction between the state and all other corporations is that the former is essentially a territorial organization, based on the primary fact of neighbourhood. According to Rousseau it is the nature of the sovereignty appertaining to the territorial community not to be capable of division. He does not distribute the rights of sovereignty among one and all of the mass of associations with which society is honeycombed. Particular associations, he claims, being always subordinate to that which contains them, one should obey the latter in the event of a conflict of loyalties.[4] He

[1] *id.*, ii. 43 : *Con. soc.*, II. iii.
[2] *id.*, i. 242.
[3] A. Mestre, 'La notion de la personalité morale chez Rousseau', *Revue du droit public*, 1902, xviii. 452.
[4] *Pol. Writings*, i. 243 : *Écon. pol.*

insists that the right of sovereignty, that is, the power of making laws binding on the whole community, must be usurped by no partial groups and belongs only to the community as a whole. Doubtless there are complications in this question of which Rousseau did not dream. It may well be asked if the individual can do without the protection partial associations afford him. Certainly Rousseau has not said the last word on this difficult problem. Nevertheless, so far as it goes, his reasoning is sound enough, and is directed as much to the assertion of the rights of the individual against the tyranny of petty corporations or powerful factions as to the assertion of the power of the state.

In general, we may conclude that Rousseau does not deny to associations the right to exist and to regulate their own affairs. When he uses the term sovereignty it is in a sense very different from that of the Austinians, who recognized the existence only of such associations as were definitely created by the law; and from that of the Jacobins, who—at least in theory—allowed subordinate associations no place at all in the state. Rousseau's fear is of those associations whose pressure can give an unfair bias to the legislative power, whose interests are divorced from those of the rest of the community, and which indeed often exist merely for the purpose of exercising an illegitimate influence over the trend of legislation. It has very truly been pointed out that here we have as explicit a condemnation as could be desired of the revolutionary clubs, and in particular of the Jacobins. The employment of his argument by the revolutionaries against the *ancien régime*, and their failure to remark its even clearer application to their own practices is characteristic of the use made of Rousseau's theories during the revolution.

4. THE CIVIL RELIGION

To deal, even summarily, with the Civil Religion, demands more space. Rousseau's starting-point in this connection seems to be the logical difficulty presented to his, as to any other theory of sovereignty, by the existence of the churches, particularly the Church of Rome, which, he argues, by giving men two legislators, two sovereigns, almost two fatherlands, renders them liable to contradictory duties, and presents them with the possibility of having to choose, sooner or later, between being faithful to their religion or loyal to their state.[1] In the endeavour to escape from this duality of power, he continues, the rulers of England and Russia have made themselves nominally heads of national churches, but have in fact merely succeeded in becoming the servants of their priests. It is significant that there is no direct reference to the Calvinist system in Rousseau's analysis of the various forms of religious organization. The reason may be, as is suggested in *Jean-Jacques Rousseau genevois*, that his civil religion is in effect the system of Calvinist Geneva without its dogmas.[2] Certainly the Calvinist church-state is the only one which escapes in some degree his condemnation, for his primary object in desiring the abolition of existing churches is to free the state from a relationship which he regards as necessarily involving the anarchy of a dual sovereignty.

The argument which Rousseau uses against the churches is precisely that which we have just seen him applying to other associations. Believing in the legislative sovereignty of the community as a whole, he could hardly with consistency allow a partial association such as a church the right of laying down general rules affecting the life of the community, for instance, the laws of probate, of marriage and divorce, or of literary censorship. Rousseau fears the situation arising when a church, acknowledging certain principles on such matters, comes into conflict with a civil state attempting to enforce different rules, and he congratulates Hobbes on having dared to propose by reuniting the 'two heads of the eagle' to bring back political unity.[3] The conflict was bound to come with the development of the modern state. It existed, indeed, under the *ancien régime*, but though there might be temporary quarrels, in the last resort divine right monarchy was dependent on the religious sanction; and even though in both Protestant and Catholic countries the church had been made politically subservient to the state, it had only been at the price of leaving large areas of conduct under its control.

Criticisms of Rousseau's civil religion are apt to be based on an implicit supposition that it is a theory peculiar to himself. On the contrary, as was shown by Mathiez, the idea that the church

[1] *Pol. Writings*, ii. 126: *Con. soc.*, IV. viii.
[2] Valette, *op. cit.*, pp. 199-206.
[3] *Pol. Writings*, ii. 127: *Con. soc.*, IV. viii.

D

should be under the state was common to practically all the *philosophes*,[1] including even Montesquieu, for whom indeed the truth of a religion seemed distinctly less important than its social utility.[2] None of the *philosophes*, and among the physiocrats only Turgot and Dupont de Nemours, envisaged the possibility of enfranchising the churches to any extent from the control of the state. Voltaire simply expressed the common opinion when he proclaimed, 'C'est insulter la raison et les lois de prononcer ces mots: *Gouvernement civil et ecclésiastique. Il faut dire gouvernement civil et réglements ecclésiastiques; et aucun de ces règlements ne doit être fait que par la puissance civile.*'[3]

Not only did the *philosophes* believe that the church should be under the state—they also uphold the more positive conception of a state church; for, with but few exceptions, they were practically all agreed that some form of religion, however false, was necessary for the maintenance of public order and morals. Even Voltaire is not so far removed from Rousseau as one might be tempted to suppose, though the patronage he rather reluctantly extends to religion is mainly on account of its utility as an adjunct to the police, whereas Rousseau in most of his works is more concerned with its effect on the virtue of the individual than on the well-being of the state. In the *Contrat social*, however, he adopts a position nearer to that of Voltaire than is his standpoint in, for instance, the *Vicaire Savoyard*, although the two works were practically contemporaneous. Because of this contradiction the chapter on the Civil Religion by itself can represent only one aspect of his conception of the place of religion in the life of society.

The fact that Rousseau's religion is something intimately concerned with the moral development of the individual makes his influence at bottom a much more serious menace to the established order than were the attacks of Voltaire. The right of the Church to lay down the principles of social behaviour could only be challenged with any possibility of success, as has been said more than once, by something more catholic than itself, and this rival could only be the idea of the community as a whole, con-

---

[1] A. Mathiez, 'Les philosophes et la séparation de l'Église et de l'État', *Révue Historique*, 1910, ciii. 63-79.

[2] *L'Esprit des Lois*, bk. XXIV, ch. XIX.

[3] *Œuvres*, xxiv. 415: *Idées républicaines*.

ceived as the supreme authority over its own life. Although for the origins of such an attitude we have to look much earlier, the writer with whom it became a world force was certainly Rousseau. One is apt to be surprised at the constant religious attacks on Rousseau, compared with the absence of hostility on political grounds, but the churches were not so wrong in detecting in him an enemy whose theories would be fatal to their claims if they were allowed to spread.

Confining ourselves strictly to the political field, however, we have to admit that it is not easy to draw any clear distinction between Rousseau and the *philosophes*. Like him, they ignore the consideration that was to weigh most heavily with later students of politics. It is obvious that the utility of a division of the sources of authority, as a means of weakening despotic power, was not adequately appreciated in the eighteenth century. Even Montesquieu failed to apply it to the churches. On the other hand as between church and state under the Bourbon monarchy, it might be claimed that power was not so much weakened by being divided as strengthened by an alliance.

But while proclaiming the supremacy of secular interests, and ignoring the argument in favour of a division of religious and political authority, Rousseau, again like the Encyclopaedists, felt the need for some organized system of belief akin in nature to a religion, but lacking the undesirable features of existing religions. Thus he was led to propose in their place the formation of a civil religion, consisting in effect of certain 'sentiments de sociabilité', which all who wish to be members of the state must accept and for the breach of which by citizens who have accepted them the penalty is death. It would hardly be fair to sum up Rousseau's God in the terms that have been used to describe Voltaire's as a celestial gendarme; nevertheless it is clearly the social and political utility of religion that he had in mind in the *Contrat social*. Indeed the chapter on the Civil Religion originally began, 'Sitôt que les hommes vivent en société, il leur faut une religion qui les y maintienne. Jamais peuple n'a subsisté, ni ne subsistera, sans religion.'[1]

Had Rousseau accepted the intellectualist political psychology of the *philosophes* he would have left the matter here and the chief source of his quarrel with them would have been lacking.

[1] *Pol. Writings*, i. 499; cf. P.-M. Masson, *La Religion de Rousseau*, ii. 186.

But he was always acutely conscious of the emotional basis of social life. To begin with, therefore, his political religion has a vitality not to be found in the platitudes of the Encyclopaedia. Moreover, we must not forget that he is primarily a moralist and that to him the good state and the virtuous individual are equally necessary the one to the other. Now since he is unwilling—in spite of Wolmar—to allow that a man can be virtuous without religion, the result is to make religion essential to the individual as well as to the state, whence arises the possibility of conflict. It is with the political aspect of religion alone that he is concerned in the *Contrat social*, with the religion which, as Vaughan puts it, enforces one's duties to one's neighbours, in other words one's duties as a member of the state,[1] and which is 'une profession de foi purement civile'.[2] This he is unwilling to permit the churches to provide for fear partly of clerical intolerance, but still more of a divided sovereignty.

What has been rightly questioned is whether Rousseau's attempt to avoid the defect of intolerance is as successful as his solution of the other difficulty, by the concentration of religious and civil authority in the same hands. Nor can the rather unfortunate language of his chapter on the Civil Religion be explained away by pointing out that elsewhere Rousseau had denounced intolerance in no qualified terms. If I were magistrate, he wrote in the *Nouvelle Héloïse*, and the law pronounced the death penalty against atheists, I would begin by burning as such the first person to inform against another.[3] But even his letter of 1756 to Voltaire, which eloquently denounces intolerance, allows the necessity of a 'profession de foi civile'.[4] He does not there venture into details, but as Masson has observed of a rather different aspect of the religious philosophy of Rousseau, what he believed to be the religion of nature was often only the religion of his fathers; similarly his Civil Religion has an effect not so very different from that of the churches of his day, though the setting is different. Beaulavon describes it not unfairly as a sort of utilitarian intolerance substituted for dogmatic intolerance.[5]

[1] *id.*, i. 88.

[2] *id.*, ii. 132: *Con. soc.*, IV. viii.

[3] *Nouv. Hél.*, iv. 103 n.

[4] *Corr. Gén.*, ii. 320-23: to Voltaire, August 18, 1756.

[5] Beaulavon, *op. cit.*, p. 340, n. 1.

When Rousseau proscribes religions that are themselves intolerant it is possible to see the grounds of his argument. It is impossible to live in peace, he writes, with those whom one believes to be damned, which sounds plausible enough, though we may be able to say that in practice it does not seem impossible at all. Again, he alleges that when he punishes atheism with death it is not on religious grounds but for 'le mensonge devant la loi'. But although more than once he admits that the law cannot command men's beliefs, this is what, in essence, he is demanding of it. To pretend that each citizen has the possibility of considering for himself the principles of the civil religion, and if they conflict with his conscience of rejecting them and quitting the community is ridiculous, and shows that Rousseau is still not fully emancipated from an artificial conception of the state. Besides, if the elementary principles of the civil religion are essential to every state, as Rousseau believes, whither shall he who refuses to accept them fly?

In the *Lettres de la Montagne* Rousseau emphasizes certain safeguards which modify, without essentially changing, the theory of the Civil Religion as expounded in the *Contrat social*. It is, he says there, only those aspects of religion which concern public welfare and social morality, the duties of the man and the citizen, which come under the jurisdiction of the government.[1] His doctrine, he expressly adds in another place, is not that of absolute power.[2] Moreover when he puts even these aspects of religion under the state it is not the power of the executive that he understands by this, but the authority of the community, acting legislatively.[3] On the other hand, even in strictly religious matters he allows that the state may establish and prescribe for teaching in its schools those doctrines which are held by the majority—this for the sake of order and system in the public instruction. The liberty of the individual, he adds, is not hindered thereby, since no one is forced to teach in spite of himself.[4] Of the liberty of the pupils he says nothing.

It will not be fair to carry this condemnation of Rousseau too far, however. The Civil Religion constitutes one of the counts on

[1] *Œuvres*, vi. 134: *Lett. Mont.*, I.
[2] *id.*, x. 218-19: *Lett. Mont.* V.
[3] *id.*, vi. 240-1: *Lett. Mont.*, V.
[4] *id.*, vi. 159: *Lett. Mont.*, II.

which he has been most severely attacked as a prophet of revolutionary intolerance, but it has been pointed out that many aspects of the religious policy of the revolution which have been attributed to him are no more than an echo of the deism of Voltaire and the Encyclopaedists.[1] Even the civic fêtes and hymns, which seem so eminently characteristic of Rousseau, are proposed equally in the works of his greatest enemy.[2] Of Robespierre and Rousseau, Masson concludes that in religious ideas, 'Les deux hommes marchent sur la même route'.[3] It is all the more interesting to see that even Robespierre was compelled on one occasion to protest against the application of Rousseau's doctrines. In a discussion at the Jacobin Club on May 15, 1794, of a proposal to denounce as traitors all professed atheists, he argued, 'Il y a des vérités qu'il convient de présenter avec ménagement, telle cette vérité proclamée par Rousseau, que ceux qui ne croient pas à la divinité doivent être bannis de la République. Je ne suis pas d'avis qu'on les proscrive tous, mais seulement ceux qui conspirent contre la liberté. . . . Il faut laisser cette vérité dans les écrits de Rousseau et ne pas la mettre en pratique.'[4] If one is looking for examples of religious intolerance in the revolution there are other illustrations than Robespierre, and among statesmen who can in no way be accused of being particularly disciples of Rousseau.

To return to the Civil Religion, one might be tempted to suppose that Rousseau's ideal is represented by the state religions of the ancient world, and certainly one cannot but detect in this case as in many other respects the influence on him of the city state. It happens, however, that he has himself specifically ruled out the religions of the ancient world, as superstitious, tyrannical, exclusive and sanguinary. One cannot help wondering what he would have said of his own Civil Religion had he ever seen it in practice. He evidently never grasped what the system he was proposing meant, for, ironically enough, he concludes the chapter on the Civil Religion with an eloquent denunciation of intolerance.

[1] A. Aulard, *Histoire politique de la Révolution française*, 5th ed., 1921, p. 646.
[2] Masson, *op. cit.*, iii. 233.
[3] *id.*, iii. 239.
[4] Quoted by E. Champion, *Jean-Jacques Rousseau et la Révolution française*, 1909, p. 234.

The difference between the Civil Religion as depicted in the *Contrat social* and Christianity in any form is striking and not merely accidental, for it reappears in the *Gouvernement de Pologne* and is commented on frequently by Rousseau himself. In his political observations on Christianity he adopts—incongruously enough—the pose of a Roman of the old school. It is a religion for slaves, for men who in this world have no fatherland.[1] The same doctrine is repeated in the Letter to Usteri of 1763,[2] and in even bolder terms in the first *Lettre de la Montagne*, where he says of Christianity what he has formerly said of the churches, that it destroys the unity of the body politic.[3] One can see why in his own time the author of the *Vicaire Savoyard* aroused such violent religious hostility. His share in the revival of religious emotions notwithstanding, he never treats religion as a good in itself but always has in mind either its moral effects on the individual or its political effects on society, and in connection with the latter he cannot hide from himself the fact that Christianity is the enemy of patriotism. Christian charity, he tells Usteri, does not permit us to draw a distinction between our fellow-countrymen and foreigners: it is suited for the making neither of republicans nor of warriors.[4]

Yet where he speaks of the influence of religion over the individual his tone is entirely different. We may try to explain this by saying that in the *Emile*, for instance, he is treating religion only as a spiritual force and not as taking the form of an organized church. But indeed he is faced, as he recognizes himself, with an insuperable difficulty. 'La science du salut' is one thing and that of government another.[5] Since all human institutions are based on human passions and maintained by them, a religion of which the object is to combat and destroy the passions, he argues, is not appropriate to strengthening these institutions.[6] True Christianity is for Rousseau an approximation to the religion of nature; therefore, though it can play a useful part in moderating human passions, if it were accepted

---

[1] *Pol. Writings*, ii. 130, 131: *Con. soc.*, IV. viii.
[2] *id.*, ii. 166.
[3] *id.*, ii. 171.
[4] *id.*, ii. 166.
[5] *id.*, ii. 172: *Lett. Mont.*, I.
[6] *id.*, ii. 170: *Lett. Mont.*, I.

in its entirety it would destroy the state.[1] We should remember, in fairness to Rousseau, that, as Masson has observed, the criticism of Christianity on political grounds was almost a commonplace among the *philosophes*. On this, as on many other points, he was more one with his enemies than either he or they supposed.

There we must leave the matter: Rousseau hardly makes any attempt to reconcile religion as a political force with what he admits to be the good religion for the individual and for humanity. This has rightly been regarded as the sphere in which he calls on the individual to make the greatest sacrifices to the state of which he is a member, though it is only just to say that they are hardly greater than Locke demands in the *Essay on Toleration*. The object of Rousseau was to free the individual from the tyranny of a caste of priests and subject him only to those religious principles which were dictated by the nature and necessities of the state itself. But, in the end, one cannot pretend to regard the chapter on the Civil Religion as other than unfortunate: though so short, more than any other section of his political writings it helps us to understand why its author should have been so often regarded as the apostle of tyranny and an enemy to liberty in the state.

5. THE ABSTRACT NATURE OF THE CONTRAT SOCIAL

If we have no more than the arguments derived from his observations on associations and the Civil Religion we have hardly adequate grounds for maintaining that Rousseau upholds the despotism of the state, in the face of his many positive pronouncements against despotic rule of any kind. Appeal can be made, however, not only to these two particular issues, but to the whole conception of the state embodied in the *Contrat social*. Before going on to this broader issue, a preliminary consideration has to be discussed. The *Contrat social* is primarily an analysis of the idea of sovereignty and the ideal state: it is, it may be said, essentially theoretical, as he put it, merely the abstract part of the bigger and more comprehensive treatise on political institutions that he at one time intended to write. Its author himself described it as a book confined to general theory on the

[1] Masson, *op. cit.* ii 183-4.

foundations of government. It was, he wrote, 'Un livre où l'on n'examine les gouvernements que par leurs principes et par les conséquences nécessaires de ces principes', adding that therefore it could have no application to any particular government which was not equally applicable to all other governments of the same kind.[1] The fact that he subsequently allows questions of expediency rather than right to creep in and goes into details of constitutional arrangements, as well as his failure to explain whether the contract itself is an historical or a philosophical conception, has partially obscured the abstract basis of his study. It must be added that the intermingling of considerations derived from abstract principle with those based on expediency, is not to be attributed to unawareness of the importance of the distinction, as is made clear by his observation concerning Montesquieu that, 'Il n'eut garde de traiter des principes du droit politique; il se contenta de traiter du droit positif des gouvernements établis; et rien au monde n'est plus différent que ces deux études'.[2]

One should not, of course, see here any justification of Faguet's view that the Contrat social was conceived as a refutation of Montesquieu.[3] On the contrary, its author was always willing to admit that facts were stubborn things and to treat questions of practical politics from the point of view of expediency. Even in the Contrat social itself he allowed that every state must have not the constitution that is best in itself, but that which is best suited to the state for which it is destined.[4] Again, one could hardly ask for anything more explicit than a passage in the Lettre à d'Alembert: 'L'homme est un, je l'avoue; mais l'homme modifié par les religions, par les gouvernements, par les lois, par les coutumes, par les préjugés, par les climats, devient si différent de lui-même, qu'il ne faut plus chercher parmi nous ce qui est bon aux hommes en général, mais ce qui leur est bon dans tel temps ou dans tel pays'.[5] A government, the best in certain circumstances, may be, he believes, the worst in others.[6] As, finally, he says in the letter to the Marquis de Mirabeau, 'La science du

---

[1] Corr. Gén., vii. 256: to M.-M. Rey, May 29, 1762.
[2] Pol. Writings, ii. 147: Émile, V.
[3] Faguet, La Politique comparée, etc., p. 59.
[4] Pol. Writings, ii. 62: Con. soc., II. ix.
[5] Œuvres, vi. 442: Lett. à d'Alembert; cf. Pol. Writings, ii. 205.
[6] Pol. Writings, ii. 157: Émile, V.

gouvernement n'est qu'une science de combinaisons, d'applications et d'exceptions, selon les temps, les lieux, les circonstances'.[1]

If Rousseau admits all this then certainly he cannot deny the necessity for a study of actual working institutions such as Montesquieu attempted, nor indeed does he. He had a weakness for striking phrases, and of the phrase with which he began the *Discours sur l'inégalité* — 'Ecarter tous les faits' — one might almost say that it has distorted the whole interpretation of his thought. But, as Hubert explains, the facts which he wishes to put on one side are those of the book of Genesis, and with this accomplished, 'Voilà donc le problème transposé sur le plan positif et historicoethnographique'. The point of view, he adds, becomes definitely that of a kind of sociological darwinism.[2] Such a standpoint was not so rare in the eighteenth century as one is sometimes tempted to suppose. Even the mathematician, d'Alembert, concedes in the *Encyclopédie* that morals, public law and history belong in a certain sense to 'experimental philosophy', and demands the establishment of chairs for their teaching as such.[3] Hence, incidentally, the great taste of the eighteenth century for collections of voyages with descriptions of foreign and barbaric manners and customs, for constitutional studies, both of England and of France, and for medieval histories, again with special reference to constitutional antecedents.

In Rousseau this tendency is well represented. The *Discours sur l'inégalité* is packed with references to the actual accounts of historians and of travellers.[4] The *Lettres de la Montagne* form a study of the operation of a particular constitution in the special environment of Geneva and are practical both in origin and in aim. The *Constitution de Corse* and even more the *Gouvernement de Pologne* provide a thorough illustration of the application of what one might call sociological methods to political problems. Vaughan draws an unnecessary distinction in so far as he compares Rousseau's earlier 'abstract' political thinking with such examples of the method of Montesquieu as are provided by the *Poland* and the *Corsica*.[5] On the contrary, the same

---

[1] *Pol. Writings*, ii. 159: *Lett. à Mirabeau*, 1767.
[2] R. Hubert, *Rousseau et l'Encyclopédie* (1742-56), 1928, p. 89.
[3] *Encyclopédie*, art. 'Experimental'.
[4] *cf.* J. Morel, 'Les sources du Discours sur l'origine de l'inégalité', in *Annales de la Soc. J.-J. Rousseau*, v.
[5] *Pol. Writings*, i. 79.

trend can be distinguished in his mind almost from the beginning of his career as a writer on politics. It is true, as Vaughan also says, that the abstract and the concrete strands are curiously intermingled in his thought,[1] but this fact in itself suggests that perhaps it is possible to trace a more intimate connection between them.

Though it is not always easy for the reader to discover whether Rousseau is dealing with the practical or the ideal, the fact should not be attributed to any fundamental confusion in his ideas. The charge of confusing the ideal with the actual, the kingdom of God with the kingdoms of this earth, is one which is made—not without justification—against some of the Idealist philosophers, but from which Rousseau was altogether exempt. He was too profoundly pessimistic to have much hope of seeing his ideal state realized on earth. His ignorance of classical conditions allowed him, like many of his contemporaries, to idealize the city states of the ancient world—all the more easily because his political ideals were themselves derived largely from classical sources. But in modern times, except for a few small states such as Geneva or Corsica, he has little hope of seeing any approximation to the principles of the Social Contract, failing which, he fears, 'perfect Hobbism' or the government of sheer force is the only practicable alternative.[2] Seek out, his tutor instructs Emile, a state where the laws rule; but where will you find it, where even will you find laws? Everywhere individual interest and passions usurp the dignity and the title of the laws.[3] Considering the governments of Europe in his day and in the subsequent century, it is not easy to say that he was wrong.

The objection that inevitably arises in one's mind has been anticipated by Rousseau, who puts it in the mouth of Emile. Why, he asks, if the perfect state is not made for men, should we trouble our heads about it? He troubled about it himself primarily because he had a passion for truth. 'La vérité générale et abstraite,' he wrote at the end of his life, 'est le plus précieux de tous les biens.'[4] In the Emile his reply is that right is not

[1] id., i. 77.
[2] Pol. Writings, ii. 161: Lett. à Mirabeau, 1767. Rousseau elsewhere stated that this letter was written in haste and never intended for publication, but he did not disavow its sentiments, v. Corr. Gén., xix. 90-1.
[3] Œuvres, iv. 210: Émile, V.
[4] Confessions, etc., iii. 193: Promeneur solitaire, IV.

dependent on human passions; our duty is first to discover what is right in politics. Subsequently we may examine actual circumstances to see what men have made of it, 'et vous verrez de belles choses'.[1] We must use, that is, our conception of the ideal state as a standard by which to measure actual states.

This way of looking at the *Contrat social*, as providing a scheme of values, which is abstract in so far as they are primarily concerned with general political principles and not with the modifications which may be necessary in their practical application in the circumstances of a particular state, has been summed up so admirably by Lanson that one cannot do better than quote his conclusion. 'Les principes du *Contrat* recommandent moins certaines institutions qu'une certaine manière de comprendre les institutions, quelles qu'elles soient: le *Contrat social* serait réalisé sans révolution, le jour où, dans la conscience du chef comme dans celle des sujets, vivrait l'esprit qui a dicté le Contrat. . . . L'erreur que certaines discussions du *Contrat* dénoncent, contre Montesquieu, c'est qu'il y ait des institutions intrinsèquement et nécessairement libérales.'[2] The institutions of a state, that is, are less important than the spirit in which they are worked and the intellectual principles on which they are based. The *Contrat social* is concerned primarily with the latter. In this sense it is an abstract work, but these are, after all, the really vital considerations, and influence the relationship of the state and the individual far more intimately than any matters of governmental machinery. Far from ruling out the *Contrat social* because it is abstract, we must emphasize its importance for the understanding of Rousseau's political thinking.

[1] *Pol. Writings*, ii. 158; *Émile*, V.
[2] G. Lanson, 'L'unité de la pensée de Rousseau', *Annales Soc. J.-J. Rousseau*, viii. 1-32.

CHAPTER III

LIBERTY AND THE GENERAL WILL

1. NATURAL RIGHTS AND THE SOCIAL ORDER

The central theme of the *Contrat social* is the attempt to put into political terms the concept of freedom in society. The criticism may be made that this is exactly the contrary of Rousseau's usual explanation of the origin of political society, which seems to imply a total abnegation of individual liberty. Rousseau describes, for instance, as the best institutions those 'qui savent le mieux dénaturer l'homme, lui ôter son existence absolue pour lui en donner une relative, et transporter le *moi* dans l'unité commune'.[1] It is the function of the Legislator on whom is bestowed the task of creating a people to transform the free and self-dependent individual into a fragment of the social unity, from which henceforth he is to receive his moral being, and thus, in Rousseau's own words, to mutilate his constitution as an individual.[2]

At first sight these and similar statements seem irreconcilable with any genuine conception of individual liberty. The misunderstanding arises from forgetting the assumptions with which Rousseau's political thinking commences. His argument starts from the ideas of natural man and natural rights. The liberty his theory leads him to attribute to natural man is so boundless, so absolute, that nothing but a complete change in psychological constitution can produce a capacity for political life. This is what Rousseau means when he places political society and liberty in opposition to one another, and when he says that independence and natural liberty have given place to laws and slavery and that freedom no longer exists for men.[3]

The change that Rousseau effects in the theory of Locke is not so much in his view of political society as in his theory of the state of nature; his natural society is a state of completely anarchic individual freedom. Its essential characteristic is that in

[1] *Pol. Writings*, ii. 145; *Émile*, I.
[2] *id.*, i. 324; *Fragment*; cf. *id.*, ii. 51-2; *Con. soc.*, II. vii.
[3] *id.*, i. 296: *L'etat de guerre*.

it man lives in isolation from his fellows. This assumption,
M. Derathé argues, determines the subsequent development of
Rousseau's theory.[1] It is necessary, however, to add the factor
which distinguishes man from the animals, even in the state of
nature, which is 'la faculté de se perfectionner'.[2] Though man
in the state of nature is non-social, amoral, and makes no use of
his reasoning powers, he possesses an undeveloped capacity for
morality and reason which is brought into action as a result of
life in society.[3] It is necessary to ask, therefore, how and why
man passes from the unsocial to the social state. To answer this
question M. Derathé appeals to a passage from the *Essai sur
l'origine des langues*, in which Rousseau maintains that men
became associated together largely as a result of the physical
accidents — floods, volcanic eruptions, earthquakes — which
Providence employed to force them into social life for their
mutual assistance.[4] This cataclysmic theory of the origin of
society may well seem one of the weakest links in Rousseau's
argument, which may be the reason why he never adduces it in
any of his major works. The suggestion has been put forward
that his theory might be brought into closer conformity with
modern thought by assuming that for him the state of nature
was an abstract idea, which never had any positive reality; but
to make this assumption would be to take Rousseau's thought
out of its historical setting. It is difficulty to deny that he believed
a non-social state of nature to represent the primitive condition
of the human race.

The problem Rousseau is faced with is thus quite different
from that of Locke, who had merely to provide a judge and a
sanction for an already acknowledged law: his problem is to
substitute a political system for total anarchy, to create out of
illegality the rule of law, and at the same time preserve the principle of liberty. In a sense this problem is insoluble: natural
rights. and therefore natural liberty, cannot continue to exist
after the formation of political society. Yet they are not entirely
abrogated but are rather held in abeyance. Every man on coming
of age has, according to Rousseau, the right of choosing between

---

[1] R. Derathé, *Rousseau et la science politique de son temps*, 1950, p. 134,
[2] R. Derathé, *Le Rationalisme de Rousseau*, 1948, p. 9.
[3] *id.*, p. 14.
[4] *Rousseau et la science politique*, pp. 178-9.

acceptance of the social contract and his natural liberty; if he prefers the latter then he has to leave the community in which the contract is established.[1] Moreover if the contract is broken then each individual re-enters into his original rights and recovers his natural liberty.[2]

One cannot pretend, however, that such ideas are as important for Rousseau as they were for Locke. Granted that as a result of his theory of the state of nature Rousseau is led to a plainly artificial version of the foundation of society by a social compact, the object of the latter is merely to cancel out the former. Once the state has been founded natural rights cease to function: there is no room for a declaration of the Rights of Man in Rousseau's state. 'A right against society,' says Green, 'in distinction from a right to be treated as a member of society, is a contradiction in terms.'[3] Rousseau would not express himself differently. The lawless conditions of life in the state of nature he is reluctant in the end even to describe by the word liberty: the term comes to acquire a new meaning for him, that of a life lived under the law. 'On a beau vouloir confondre l'indépendance et la liberté. Ces deux choses sont si différentes que même elles s'excluent mutuellement. Quand chacun fait ce qu'il lui plaît, on fait souvent ce qui déplaît à d'autres; et cela ne s'appelle pas un état libre. . . . Dans la liberté commune, nul n'a droit de faire ce que la liberté d'un autre lui intérdit; et la vraie liberté n'est jamais destructive d'elle-même. La liberté sans la justice est une véritable contradiction.'[4]

It is to the law alone, he says on another occasion, that men owe justice and liberty; it is the law which establishes real equality among them, and which dictates to each citizen, 'les préceptes de la raison publique, et lui apprend à agir selon les maximes de son propre jugement, et à n'être pas en contradiction avec lui-même'.[5] This is the reason why in the *Contrat social*, so

---

[1] Such is his advice to d'Ivernois: 'C'est d'en sortir tous, tous ensemble, en plein jour, vos femmes et vos enfants au milieu de vous, et puis qu'il faut porter des fers, d'aller porter du moins ceux de quelque Grand Prince, et non pas l'insupportable et odieux joug de vos égaux'. (*Corr. Gén.*, xviii. 83 : January 29, 1768.)

[2] *Pol. Writings*, ii. 32-3 : *Con. soc.*, I. vi.

[3] T. H. Green, *Principles of Political Obligation*, § 99; *Works*, 1885 (6th impr., 1911), ii. 416.

[4] *Pol. Writings*, ii., 234-5 : *Lett. Mont.*, VIII.

[5] *id.*, i. 245 : *Écon. pol.*

often taken as the very gospel of *étatisme*, is to be found a paean to the cause of liberty which on any such interpretation of the work is quite inexplicable. 'Renoncer à sa liberté,' he writes, 'c'est renoncer à sa qualité d'homme, aux droits d'humanité, même à ses devoirs. . . . Une telle renonciation est incompatible avec la nature de l'homme; et c'est ôter toute moralité à ses actions que d'ôter toute liberté à sa volonté.'[1] In the *Discours sur l'inégalité*, almost in the same terms, he had written that liberty was the noblest faculty of man, and that to renounce the most precious of all his gifts would be to degrade his own nature, to put himself on a level with the beasts enslaved to their instincts, and to commit a crime against the very author of his being.[2]

Rousseau's chief object is to discover some means by which, in return for sacrificing the absolute independence, the freedom from all but physical needs of the state of nature, the individual shall gain in political society the capacity for moral liberty, and this he finds in the *Contrat social*. Although his state of nature was a state of happiness in which there was no knowledge of good or evil, and Rousseau did not feel confident that man had gained by changing this state for life in society, there was, he fully recognized, no possibility of a return to it. Once men had begun to live in society a psychological revolution had occurred which cut them off from the path back, as ineluctably as the angel with the flaming sword barred Adam and Eve from the road back to Eden. With the beginning of social life appear new problems and new passions of which man had been innocent before. Rousseau does not accept Hobbes's identification of the natural principle of self-preservation with a restless and unlimited pride. It is only after men have begun to live in society that the aggressive passions which lead to a state of war and mutual hostility appear, and natural pity or *bonté naturelle*, which had moved natural man in his rare and transient contacts with his fellows, ceases to be adequate to protect him from the consequences of his own passions. Their tyranny is now only to be conquered by the new force of *vertu*, which itself is made possible by the growth of the human reason. M. Derathé decisively rejects the common condemnation of Rousseau as an irrationalist, for whom human reason is inherently corrupt.

[1] *id.*, ii. 28: *Con. soc.*, I. iv.
[2] *id.*, i. 186: *Disc. inég.*

Rousseau's law of nature is in fact the law of reason; innate in natural man, it develops, as his reason develops, with social life, outside which morality, reason, and therefore liberty are inconceivable.[1] To put it in Rousseau's own words, 'Ce passage de l'état de nature à l'état civil produit dans l'homme un changement très remarquable, en substituant dans sa conduite la justice à l'instinct, en donnant à ses actions la moralité qui leur manquait auparavant. . . . Son âme toute entière s'élève à tel point que, si les abus de cette nouvelle condition ne le dégradaient souvent au-dessous de celle dont il est sorti, il devrait bénir sans cesse l'instant heureux qui l'en arracha pour jamais, et qui, d'un animal stupide et borné, fit un être intelligent et un homme.'[2]

With Rousseau politics, as a quotation such as the last shows, is but a branch of morals: its object is to develop the individual as a moral being and to enable him to live a good life. Vaughan described the *Discours sur l'inégalité* as the work of a moralist rather than a political theorist, but indeed the two roles are hardly to be distinguished in Rousseau. His employment of the contractual theory has been presented in terms of a moral history of humanity. 'Sans le contrat, l'histoire humaine n'est que le récit d'une longue déchéance, et le pessimisme triomphe. Mais le contrat est l'instrument du salut de l'humanité. C'est parce qu'il peut être conçu qu'il est ordonné de croire à la bonté originelle et positive de la nature humaine. C'est par lui que la justice naît et que la moralité devient accessible à l'homme.'[3] In other words, adds the same critic, Rousseau's contractual theory is a transposition into historical experience of the traditional religious theory of the Fall and the Salvation.

The process by which man moves from the natural state to civil society is a mighty step: it is a revolution in human life, for it is at this point that man becomes a moral and political animal. Rousseau's realization of the supreme importance of the change, which he embodied in the social contract, led him to the discovery, announced in the *Confessions*, that 'tout tenait radicalement à la politique'.[4] It was a discovery that his predecessors

---

[1] *Rousseau et la science politique*, pp. 133, 164-8, 176; *Le Rationalisme de Rousseau*, pp. 3-4, 157, 168.

[2] id., ii. 36: *Con. soc.*, I. viii.

[3] Hubert, *op. cit.*, p. 133.

[4] *Confessions*, liv. IX.

E

could not have made, for it was only in the eighteenth century that it began to be true, with the emancipation of government from the restraints that had formerly bound it, and the beginning of the age in which political power for the first time acquired almost universal scope. The word sovereignty was to come to mean much more than it had formerly meant, precisely because the fact of sovereignty began to mean much more. Because political power was now the basis of all power, Rousseau was right in holding that political liberty was the basis of all other liberties. His political theory can be described as an attempt to come to grips with the new fact of unlimited sovereignty, to recognize its existence, and at the same time reconcile it with liberty.

In his rather touching faith in the power of laws and institutions to create moral freedom and virtue Rousseau is a man of his age. More typical of his own inner feelings are his occasional hesitations, as when he breaks out in the *Emile* with, 'La liberté n'est dans aucune forme de gouvernement, elle est dans le cœur de l'homme libre, il la porte partout avec lui'.[1] Or, as he writes to d'Ivernois, 'Il n'y a plus de liberté sur la terre que dans le cœur de l'homme juste'.[2] Rousseau, as the author of parts of the Second Discourse and the prophet of the romantics, cannot but regret the loss of absolute personal independence, but as a political theorist and a moralist he realizes its inevitability. A conflict exists in his mind, as Vaughan has said, between his consciousness that society is the necessary medium of man's full realization of himself as a moral being, and his own hatred of social obligations, his almost pathological craving for personal independence. Even so we must not exaggerate his devotion to abstract liberty. 'Je n'ai jamais cru,' he wrote, 'que la liberté de l'homme consistât à faire ce qu'il veut, mais bien à ne jamais faire ce qu'il ne veut pas.'[3]

In existing conditions his prescription for the individual who wishes to live a virtuous life is to withdraw from the company of his fellows, to leave a corrupt society to its fate and to fall back on the inner resources of his own nature, in which he will find reflected the essential goodness of original nature, un-

---

[1] *Œuvres*, v. 433: *Émile*, V.

[2] *Corr. Gén.*, xviii. 82: to d'Ivernois, January 29, 1768.

[3] *Confessions*, etc., iii. 230: *Promeneur solitaire*, VII.

corrupted by a degenerate race of men. Such is the source of the individualism of the second *Discours* and the *Emile*.

Rousseau does not blame the innate constitution of human nature for the evil he sees around him: he attributes it rather to the selfishness of those classes who found it to their interest to raise and maintain corrupt institutions. It follows from his way of looking at the situation that if bad institutions could corrupt those who lived under them, for the mass of men, who could not —as could Emile or the *Promeneur solitaire*—escape from the evil influences of society by isolating themselves, the only means of achieving virtue was with the aid of new and better social and political institutions. 'J'avais vu,' he wrote, 'que tout tenait radicalement à la politique, et que, de quelque façon qu'on s'y prît, aucun peuple ne serait que ce que la nature de son gouvernement le ferait être.' [1] Consequently, in the reform of the individual, virtue, although the very stuff of uncorrupted human nature, has to be re-created by the action of political institutions. To sum up, according to Rousseau's way of looking at the question, the isolated individual in the state of nature is virtuous, society brings corruption, from which, since there is no returning to the state of nature, the only escape lies through the action of political institutions, definitely planned to create anew an environment in which virtue becomes possible. To the state, thus, is attributed an ethical function in the life of the individual, and the result is to create a bond between the state, or society, and the individual far stronger than the mere utilitarian connection.

One cannot doubt that as his political ideas matured Rousseau came to hold a positive conception which in comparison with the ideas of the time seemed to and did in fact make the individual much more one with the state. Such a sympathetic critic of Rousseau as Vaughan goes even farther, declaring that in the end Rousseau reduces the individual to a cypher in the state. He sums up the *Contrat social* as 'the porch to a collectivism as absolute as the mind of man has ever conceived'.[2] It is not fair to take this for granted, however; the effect on political liberty of a closer connection between the individual and the state can be judged only after a detailed examination of the nature of that connection.

[1] *Confessions, etc.,* ii. 241: bk. IX.
[2] *Pol. Writings,* i. 39; cf. *id.,* i. 56, 59.

A favourite argument of those who in the nineteenth century tried to subject the individual entirely to the state was the parallel with an organic body, and upholders of the organic theory of society have looked back to Rousseau, as to Burke, for support. In so far as these two thinkers played a large part in overthrowing the influence on political thought of the individualism of the school of Locke, it is possible to regard them in such a light. But this should not prevent us from recognizing the fact that Rousseau, as well as Burke, expressly repudiates the analogy between the state and an animal organism.[1]

At first sight he does not appear consistent in his observations in this connection, and a passage of the *Economie politique* certainly utilizes the analogy between the state and the human body.[2] But any attempt to interpret the parallel as more than a useful analogy is specifically ruled out in the *Contrat social*. 'Les hommes,' he says there, 'ne peuvent engendrer de nouvelles forces, mais seulement unir et diriger celles qui existent.'[3] There can be no other meaning attached to another sentence, 'Mais, outre la personne publique, nous avons à considérer les personnes privées qui la composent, et dont la vie et la liberté sont naturellement indépendentes d'elle'.[4] Again, he says, 'La constitution de l'homme est ouvrage de la nature; celle de l'Etat est l'ouvrage de l'art'.[5] Finally, to put an end to these citations, the *Etat de guerre* excludes the organic theory in so many words, 'La différence de l'art humain à l'ouvrage de la nature se fait sentir dans ses effets. Les citoyens ont beau s'appeler membres de l'Etat, ils ne sauraient s'unir à lui comme de vrais membres le sont au corps; il est impossible de faire que chacun d'eux n'ait pas une existence individuelle et séparée, par laquelle il peut seul suffire à sa propre conservation.'[6]

Locke explains himself no differently. If the end of the eighteenth century marks the watershed between the individualism of the school of Locke and the organic theories of the nineteenth century, there can be no question on which side

[1] cf. A. Cobban, *Edmund Burke and the Revolt against the Eighteenth Century*, 2nd ed. 1960, pp. 89-91.
[2] Pol. Writings, i. 241.
[3] id., ii. 32: Con. soc., I. vi.
[4] id., ii. 43-4: Con. soc., II. iv.
[5] id., ii. 91: Con. soc., III. xi.
[6] id., i. 298.

Rousseau is to be found. A later idealist, Bosanquet, frankly recognized that in Rousseau's thought there is a hard core of individualism. 'He is appealing,' he writes, 'from the organized life, institutions, and selected capacity of a nation to that nation regarded as an aggregate of isolated individuals.'[1] To attempt to read the theories of those thinkers who in the nineteenth century endeavoured to build up an organic theory of the state back into Rousseau is a perversion of his thought. And as he has taken so much trouble to make his meaning clear in this respect it is surely ungrateful not to allow him to be the intepreter of his own ideas.

Since the first edition of this book was published, this interpretation has been strongly supported by M. Derathé, who agrees that Rousseau remained a man of his age in clinging to individualism and refusing to set up any super-individual as the end of social life, and that analogies between the state and the human body in Rousseau's writings are only incidental metaphors,[2] that his natural man lives in a condition of extreme individualism, and that the formation of civil society is a voluntary act on the part of the individuals who come together to conclude the social contract. Vaughan was led into his organic interpretation of Rousseau's political theory, first because he treated the Rousseauist picture of the state of nature as a mere 'picturesque introduction', of no real significance for Rousseau's mature thought; and secondly because he interpreted Rousseau's description of the state as an *être moral* in the light of nineteenth-century ideas, and not as the term would have been taken in Rousseau's own day. M. Derathé deals with both points decisively. He shows clearly that Rousseau's conception of natural man gave an individualist bent to the whole development of his thought,[3] and that in the idea of the state as an *être moral*, or *corps artificiel*, Rousseau was merely borrowing an idea which was a commonplace of the Natural Law jurists, and employing it in exactly the same sense, to signify a political or social entity with only 'an abstract and collective existence'.[4]

[1] B. Bosanquet, *Philosophical Theory of the State*, 3rd ed., 1920, pp. 108-9.
[2] *Rousseau et la science politique*, Appendix IV, pp. 410-13.
[3] *Rousseau et la science politique*, pp. 130-1.
[4] *id.*, pp. 238, 369, Appendix III, pp. 397-410.

Not only in the form of the organic theory, but wherever he meets the point of view that would subordinate the welfare of individuals as such to some supposed greater good of the state, Rousseau's opposition is manifest. Thus Helvétius, 'Tout devient légitime et même verteux pour le salut public': on which favourite superficiality Rousseau descends with crushing force in the note, 'Le salut public n'est rien, si tous les particuliers ne sont en sûreté'.[1] In the *Economie politique* he limits the rights of the state in the clearest manner possible. 'Si l'on entend qu'il soit permis au Gouvernement de sacrifier un innocent au salut de la multitude, je tiens cette maxime pour une des plus exécrables que jamais la tyrannie ait inventées.'[2]

Although Rousseau introduces new elements into existing political theory, then, he is too much a man of the eighteenth century to discard individualism; and he is equally one with his contemporaries in his acceptance of the principle of utility. His explanation of the object of society is the utilitarian one. 'C'est ce qu'il y a de commun dans ces différents intérêts qui forme le lien social; et s'il n'y avait pas quelque point dans lequel tous les intérêts s'accordent, nulle société ne saurait exister.'[3] It follows too, that when the individuals regard their own interest as separate and different from that of the rest of the community the state is threatened with dissolution.[4] This is, of course, a commonplace. It would be difficult to find a political philosopher before the nineteenth century who proposed any other end for the state than the common good. Since he does not conceive of the state or society as a super-individual, to the supposed interests of which those of the individuals composing it must be sacrificed, it follows that the common good is for Rousseau identified with the welfare of the individual members of the state. Thus he is able to conclude, 'Le droit que le pacte social donne au souverain sur les sujets ne passe point, comme je l'ai dit, les bornes de l'utilité publique', and to supplement this with a quotation from d'Argenson, 'Dans la République chacun est parfaitement libre en ce qui ne nuit pas aux autres'.[5] We are nearer to John Stuart Mill than we should have supposed.

[1] *Œuvres* (ed. of 1826), xi. 159 n.
[2] *Pol. Writings*, i. 252.
[3] *id.*, ii. 39-40: *Con. soc.*, II. i.
[4] *id.*, ii. 103: *Con. soc.*, IV. i.
[5] *id.*, ii. 131: *Con. soc.*, IV. viii.

While Rousseau accepts in this sense an individualist and utilitarian end, utility is not the only object he prescribes for political society. At the very outset of the *Contrat social* he brings us face to face with the two elements in his political ideal. 'Je tâcherai,' he says, 'd'allier toujours, dans cette recherche, ce que le droit permet avec ce que l'intérêt prescrit, afin que la justice et l'utilité ne se trouvent point divisées.'[1] This duality is reflected in his whole theory of the end of the state: if the latter can be given a utilitarian end it is because utilitarianism is itself one aspect of social justice.

2. THE SOVEREIGNTY OF THE GENERAL WILL

The problem of uniting justice and utility in the state is, as Rousseau says in so many words at the outset, the theme of *Du Contrat social*. Implied in his argument is one basic assumption, however, which he does not discuss because he takes it for granted. The fundamental ideas of any period, of course, are those which are so widely accepted that no one thinks of questioning them. In the second half of the eighteenth century the idea of the sovereignty of the state was such an idea. Every state, says Rousseau, requires a sovereign, and he adds, 'Il est de l'essence de la puissance souveraine de ne pouvoir être limitée: elle peut tout, ou elle n'est rien'.[2] However extreme this may sound, all it means is that in every state there must be a law-making power, and that the power which makes the law must logically be above the law, in other words must be sovereign. Moreover, though Rousseau permits no other social force to challenge the sovereign, he hardly does himself justice in describing it as an unlimited power, for in fact it is limited by the terms of its own definition. The validity of the criticism directed against Rousseau's, as against any other theory of sovereignty, depends on the way in which it is interpreted, and it must be recognized that his theory has features peculiar to itself.

It is sometimes suggested that there is an essential difference between Rousseau's conception of sovereignty and that of his predecessor, Locke. When the theory of the divine institution of government became discredited its place was taken by the

[1] Pol. *Writings*, ii. 23: Con. soc., I. i.
[2] *id.*, ii. 219: *Lett. Mont.*, VII.

contractual theory, according to which society itself appointed its ruler on certain conditions, these being embodied in the social compact. If the prince broke these terms he automatically forfeited his title and his powers reverted to the community, in the possession of which ultimate sovereign power resided. Sovereignty was hence kept in reserve and only called into action on rare occasions: nor must we underestimate the value of this fact as a safeguard. There are two contracts implied in Locke's theory, the one between all the individuals who agree to forsake the state of nature and form a political society, the second between the members of this society and the government or prince they set up. On the contrary, for Rousseau there is only one contract, that forming the political society, which itself constitutes the sovereign, and in the inalienable possession of which remain the rights of sovereignty.[1] Thus while for Locke the sovereignty of the people is only operative in the last resort, for Rousseau the sovereign people is the actual legislative authority of the community.

Every critic has noted Rousseau's insistence on the unitary nature of sovereignty, and its freedom from the bonds of constitutional law. M. Derathé attributes this view to the direct influence of Hobbes, to whose basic ideas, he believes, Rousseau, after having condemned them ruthlessly earlier, now returns.[2] I do not feel convinced of this. Admittedly, the description given of Rousseau's conception of sovereignty would also apply to that of Hobbes; but before accepting this interpretation it is necessary to ask whether there is no other route by which Rousseau could have reached the same idea, and whether—given its setting in the whole nexus of his thought—it is in fact the same idea. On the first point, Rousseau's line of argument is quite plain. Sovereignty is indivisible because it is the expression of the general will. It could be divided only if that will could be divided, which by definition is impossible, for in that case it would no longer be the general will.[3] Hobbes's argument for the indivisibility

[1] cf. Green op. cit., § 64; Works, ii. 386.

[2] Rousseau et la science politique, pp. 111, 338-89, 345.

[3] Pol. Writings, ii. 41 : Du Contrat social, liv. II, ch. ii. There is the further consideration that the general will is indivisible because it is a will. 'Comme la nature donne à chaque homme un pouvoir absolu sur tous ses membres, le pacte social donne au Corps politique un pouvoir absolu sur tous les siens.' Pol. Writings, ii. 43 : id., ch. iv. This power is the volonté or will.

of sovereignty is entirely different. It is that 'if the essential rights of sovereignty . . . be taken away, the commonwealth is thereby dissolved' — 'and this division is it, whereof it is said, *a kingdom* divided in itself cannot stand'. Again, 'What is it to divide the power of a commonwealth, but to dissolve it?'[1] Whereas Rousseau appeals to the nature of sovereignty, Hobbes depends on the result of dividing it. It is not too much to say that their arguments on this point nowhere meet. There is, moreover, a striking contrast between the rôle of the theory of sovereignty in the political thought of Hobbes and its function in Rousseau. Hobbes is throughout concerned to emancipate the sovereign from control or limitations of any kind. 'The sovereign power . . . is as great as possibly men can be imagined to make it.'[2] The idea that an absolute power could be limited would have seemed to him sheer nonsense. Rousseau, on the other hand, who entitles a chapter 'On the limits of the sovereign's power',[3] while he insists that the general will cannot be bound by a fundamental law or constitution, these being necessarily of its own creation, at the same time maintains that it cannot go beyond the limits of 'general conventions' and public utility.[4]

The originality of Rousseau's theory lies in the fact that for him, once it has been concluded, the social contract sinks into a place of secondary importance. It is introduced for the purpose of explaining the origin of political society, but what is really of significance is to be found in the developments that follow. So little essential is the contractual theory to his thought that in the *Economie politique*, which may be taken as the first draft of the ideas destined to be elaborated in the *Contrat social*, it plays no part at all. In this work it is not the contract but the general will which is recognized as the 'premier principe de *l'économie publique* et règle fondamentale du Gouvernement'.[5] And even in his more famous treatise his true interest is not the contract, which is rapidly passed over, but the general will, in the existence of which he finds the essential characteristic of the state.

[1] *Leviathan*, ed. Oakeshott, 1946, pp. 118-19, 213, 219-20.

[2] *id.*, p. 136.

[3] *Contrat social*, liv. II, ch. iv.

[4] *Pol. Writings*, ii. 46. *id.* Rousseau's distinction between the sovereign and the government is also to be remembered.

[5] *id.*, i. 244: *Écon. pol.*

A result of the diversion of interest from the social contract to the general will is the attribution of will to the state, which is thus brought into the realm of moral law. But whereas individual wills may be good or bad, the peculiarity of the general will is that by definition it cannot be other than good. We are introduced here to an argument that is frequently misinterpreted. The effect of Rousseau's definition of the general will, it is alleged, is to set up the doctrine that the state can do no wrong, and to justify every act performed in its name. This is to fly in the face of what Rousseau himself says. The whole constituted authorities and every individual member of the state may be agreed on a certain line of action, but he will not accept it as a valid expression of the general will unless it fulfils the conditions he has laid down, unless, that is, it is general not only in origin but also in scope, and unless it is inspired by the general and permanent interests of the community. It is not, he specifies, the number of voices that generalizes the will, but the common interest uniting them.[1]

We may ask, may not the community have immoral interests? Rousseau would reply that if it had it would be denying the very object for which it is called into existence, to make possible the good life for its citizens, and stultifying itself. Thus the state is sovereign for him only so far as it is the embodiment of social justice, and the extent to which the sovereignty of the general will can be predicated of any particular state depends on the degree of closeness with which it approximates to this ideal. This is the truth behind the accusation of Faguet that the *Contrat social* is the last of the theologico-political works of the Calvinists, and therefore naturally authoritarian.[2]

A second characteristic of Rousseau's conception of sovereignty which is often criticized is that it is inalienable and indivisible. Is the latter quality reconcilable, it will be asked, with the principle of the separation of powers? It is for Rousseau, because the 'powers' the separation of which he acknowledges to be necessary, are not component parts of the sovereign but emanations from it, and to maintain and balance these rival powers a supreme authority is, he thinks, necessary.[3] But even apart from

[1] Pol. *Writings*, ii. 45: *Con. soc.*, II. iv.
[2] Faguet, *La politique comparée*, p. 17.
[3] Pol. *Writings*, ii. 41: *Con. soc.*, II. ii.

this consideration Rousseau's claim seems to me little more than a rather elaborate way of expressing the simple fact that two contrary and opposed wills cannot each represent what is best for the community. Although we may not always be able to ascertain which is ideally the best course of action for a community in any given circumstances, that alone is entitled to claim to be the general will.

Even understood in this sense, however, the attribution to an inalienable, indivisible will of unlimited rights of sovereignty produces a force in which the attributes of the most despotic power seem to be united. Rousseau is not concerned to moderate the appearance of his doctrine. The general will must be supreme in the state and whoever refuses to obey its dictates 'y sera contraint par tout le Corps'.[1] But the practical application of these doctrines is less drastic than is often supposed, for the volitions of the general will are expressed only through the laws. In practice, we may ask, is Rousseau claiming any more than that in every state the individual members of the body politic should be compelled by the physical powers of the whole society to obey the laws rightfully established? If this idea is a mere platitude today, it none the less needed emphasizing in eighteenth-century France, when exceptions to the law were almost the rule, and when privileged classes or individuals could break the law practically with impunity. Murderers, thieves, forgers, experience the sanctions of the law in every community. So also do those who infringe any of the innumerable petty economic and social regulations which the complexities of modern industrial civilization have rendered necessary. The only method by which such compulsion can be really justified, or reconciled with any adequate idea of the extension of individual liberty, is by some such theory as that of the general will. In essence, we might claim, Rousseau's theory is no more than an attempt to solve the problem to which eighteenth-century utilitarianism had found no satisfactory solution, that of reconciling in theory the rightful claims of the individual with those of the community.

In asserting that the sovereignty of the general will was both absolute and limited, Rousseau may seem to be using the language of paradox; but for his contemporaries, as M. Derathé says, he was merely expressing a commonplace, which could

[1] Pol. Writings, ii. 36: Con. soc., I. vii.

equally well be found, for example, in Jurieu or in Burlamaqui.[1] One important restriction on sovereignty which they upheld is Natural Law itself. The view, which I formerly shared with Vaughan and many others, that Rousseau rejected the idea of Natural Law, has been shown by M. Derathé to be untenable.[2] Of course, so widely held an opinion is unlikely to have been entirely without foundation, and it is true that Rousseau objects to all existing conceptions of the Law of Nature. But if he held that there is no Law of Nature, how, M. Derathé asks, could Rousseau have provided a moral sanction for his social contract? He certainly assumes such a sanction, in the form of a prior law obliging men to keep their agreements.[3]

Although Rousseau will not allow that the general will can be limited by any fundamental law, he does not repudiate the idea of a natural law. In one place, indeed, he expressly declares that there are three authorities superior to the sovereign, that of God, that of natural law, which derives from the natural constitution of man, and the authority that the idea of honour has over honest men. The general will, of course, if it is what it must by definition be, could not conflict with any of these. It is interesting to see that Rousseau has himself noted on the original draft, 'Cette petite pièce est très bonne; il la faut employer'.[4]

We still have to ask how such an assumption is reconcilable with his description of the state of nature as a pre-moral state. It is tempting to evade the problem by explaining away the state of nature, which, it might be said, is derived by Rousseau from current political thinking, but occupies no essential place in his

---

[1] *Rousseau et la science politique*, p. 340. 'An absolute power must not be confused with a power which is arbitrary, despotic and unlimited.' Burlamaqui, *Principes du droit politique*, 1751, Première Partie, ch. viii, para. 17.

[2] *Rousseau et la science politique*, pp. 151, 155-60.

[3] *id.*, p. 160. M. Derathé identifies this obligation with Hobbes's third Law of Nature, 'That men perform their covenants made' (*Leviathan*, p. 93); but here again Hobbes's argument is quite different from that of Rousseau. The keeping of covenants can only be described as a moral obligation in Hobbes by virtue of his nice perversion of language; for covenants, he says, are void unless there is a common power over the parties to compel their performance (p. 89). Fear is what holds men to their covenants (p. 92). 'Justice, therefore, that is to say, keeping of covenants, is a rule of reason, by which we are forbidden to do anything destructive to our life; and consequently a law of nature" (p. 96). To say the least, this is a peculiar kind of moral obligation and quite different from that of Rousseau.

[4] L. J. Courtois, *Chronologie critique de J.-J. Rousseau*, 1924, p. 102.

thought. The state of nature and the social contract, it can be argued, are both formal ideas which he takes over from his predecessors merely to use the one to cancel out the other; after which he arrives at the true starting point of his thought—'man is a political animal'. The result is to restore political thinking to the plane on which the Greeks had placed it. This interpretation is, I think, not untrue, and it certainly explains neatly one of the reasons why Rousseau's political thought exercised such a great influence. But in the light of what M. Derathé says of the Natural Law jurists, it is clear that the ideas of the state of nature and the social contract were, even in the middle of the eighteenth century, far from being merely empty formulae, and that both ideas exercised a decisive influence over the development of Rousseau's thought.

Theoretically, then, the sovereignty of the general will represents an attempt to justify philosophically the rule of law. Its effect on liberty in the state will depend on the way in which the general principle is elaborated. The most important distinction which it is necessary to make before we can attempt a further revaluation of Rousseau's theory of sovereignty has been described so authoritatively by Green that we cannot do better than quote him. 'The sovereignty of which Rousseau discusses the origin and attributes, is something essentially different from the supreme coercive power which previous writers on the *jus civile* had in view. A contemporary of Hobbes had said that

> There's on earth a yet auguster thing,
> Veiled though it be, than Parliament or King.

It is to this "auguster thing", not to such supreme power as English lawyers held to be vested in "Parliament and King", that Rousseau's account of the sovereign is really applicable. What he says of it is what Plato or Aristotle might have said of the θεῖος νοῦς, which is the source of the laws and discipline of the ideal polity, and what a follower of Kant might say of the "pure practical reason", which renders the individual obedient to a law of which he regards himself, in virtue of his reason, as the author, and causes him to treat humanity equally in the person of others and in his own always as an end, never merely as a means'.[1]

[1] Green, *op. cit.*, § 68; *Works*, ii. 388.

Green gives equally forcefully the common criticism against this theory of sovereignty. 'The practical result is a vague exaltation of the prerogatives of the sovereign people, without any corresponding limitations of the conditions under which an act is to be deemed that of the sovereign people. . . . And as the will of the people in any other sense than the measure of what the people will tolerate is really unascertainable in the great nations of Europe, the way is prepared for the sophistries of modern political management, for manipulating electoral bodies, for influencing elected bodies, and procuring plebiscites.'[1] This indictment bears rather on a possible misinterpretation of Rousseau than on what he himself actually maintained. In fact the three points singled out by Green for criticism—the absence of limitation on the action of the general will, the difficulty of ascertaining the general will in large states, and the corruptness of politics in these—are all expressly denounced by Rousseau himself.

The most usual criticism is less subtle. It is assumed that the sovereignty of the general will means the sovereignty of the people, which in turn is equated to the tyranny of the majority. To quote only one of many possible illustrations we could give, one writer defines Rousseau's theory as, 'la tyrannie de Etat, c'est-à-dire dans sa doctrine, de la majorité des citoyens contre la minorité des citoyens'.[2] It is true that in the *Contrat social* Rousseau allows that when the political society was formed its members agreed to submit themselves to the will of the majority; that henceforth the voice of the greatest number must overrule the opinions of the rest,[3] and that he allows, for instance, taxation to be determined by majority vote. Nevertheless there is a difference between agreeing in a democratic society to abide by the verdict of the majority, and attributing to that verdict the whole sovereignty of the state. According to Rousseau the claim to rightful sovereignty is determined by the nature of the particular majority will, which can only be sovereign if it possesses all the attributes necessary by definition to the general will.[4]

Far from being open to the charge of identifying the will of

[1] *id.*, § 69; *Works*, ii. 388-9.
[2] A. Dide, *J.-J. Rousseau, le protestantisme et la Révolution française*, p. 165.
[3] *Pol. Writings*, ii. 105: *Con. soc.*, IV. ii.
[4] *id.*, ii. 106: *Con. soc.*, IV. ii.

the sovereign with that of the majority, one might almost claim that Rousseau is one of the few modern authors whose theory of government is immune from it. He even admits the possibility that the general will may be embodied not merely in the will of a minority but in that of a single man, the Legislator—though this last only seems possible to him in the initial phase of the life of the state. When the laws appropriate to the circumstances of the state have been enunciated by the Legislator Rousseau seems to assume that the state, if it be in a healthy condition and destined to flourish, will recognize them as such and accept them as the expression of its true general will. Here he strays far from the nineteenth-century idea of democratic government; and it is not Rousseau but Locke, who without question gives the right of law making to the majority and only limits it by demanding that the forms of the constitution be observed. Again, practically all other supporters of the theory of the sovereignty of the people accept the representative system and thus pass on to a mere majority not of the people, but of an assembly, the whole of the immense right of sovereignty.

Rousseau is more successful in coping with the theoretical problem that he set himself than Green allows. The self-contradiction supposed in his theory is non-existent. Green argues, 'Upon the theory of the foundation of legitimate sovereignty in consent, the theory that the natural right of the individual is violated unless he is himself a joint imponent of the law which he is called to obey, it is not easy to see what rightful claim there can be to the submission of a minority'.[1] But, as I have said, the majority is sovereign only if its will is also the general will, in which are embodied the interests of the society as a whole. For it is important to bear in mind that Rousseau closely associates will and interests. He does not allow that any individual or community can have a *real* will which is fundamentally opposed to its real and permanent interests.

When we pass from pure theory to practical questions, of course, difficulties at once arise. To say that the general will embodies the interests of the community as a whole does not take us very far in practice. It is as well to confess at once that Rousseau's definition is rather intangible. If we demand a more positive description we are put off with the statement that the

[1] Green, *op. cit.*, § 75; *Works*, ii. 394.

general will embodies the will of the people, that it is, in Rousseau's own words, 'l'organe sacré de la volonté d'un peuple'. Given the qualifications with which he surrounds his idea of the general will, this is meaningless verbiage; nevertheless, taken quite literally, the definition became the favourite one of democrats during the subsequent century. It was only to be expected that practical politicians should seize on the one definite concrete point in Rousseau's system that they could understand and neglect the qualifications, though the latter are in truth the essence of the doctrine.

To sum up, as has been said, the general will, being indivisible and inalienable, is therefore incapable of being represented or of being attributed, along with the power of sovereignty, to any governing body as such. It is also a will that is always in the interests of the society as a whole and that cannot err. For other political theorists also the sovereign is incapable of error; but whereas for them this quality of the sovereign arises from the very fact of its existence, for Rousseau the existence of the sovereign itself depends on the quality of its will. It follows from all these considerations that there are necessarily many states without a general will, that is, without a rightful sovereign. Green, indeed, says that hardly any state can be legitimate on Rousseau's principles, but that depends on what one means by legitimacy. Rousseau, as I have said, does not in practice question the legitimacy of any established authority. It has been said of him that he wished to make even monarchy accepted, though he only succeeded in making the Republic loved. On the other hand, it is true that most governments being founded on tyranny and corruption few or none were legitimate from the point of view of the ideal state—and one must always remember that this was Rousseau's point of view in the *Contrat social*.

The general will may be endowed by Rousseau with limitless sovereignty, but its existence as he understood it, and therefore the legitimate exercise of sovereignty, demands not only a tiny state in which all the people may express their will without the intervention of a representative system, and a constitution which puts the legislative power in the hands of the people, but also a permanent desire on their part to pursue only the common good, together with sufficient enlightenment to know how to put the desire into practice. We may be in the land of Utopias:

we are certainly a long way from that absolutism of the state which became one interpretation of Rousseau.

3. SEPARATION OF POWERS

Among the other particular arguments which, apart from its general philosophical tendency, have led to the interpretation of the *Contrat social* as a justification of the despotic state, must be mentioned the belief that it is hostile to the separation of powers, a system identified, through the influence of Montesquieu, with political liberty. This interpretation of Rousseau is based either on a single quotation from the *Contrat social*,[1] which is not altogether relevant, or else on his attribution to the legislative power of a right of inspection over the executive which is equally permitted in the *Esprit des Lois* itself.[2]

The passage to which reference is usually made is that in which he criticizes those who would divide the sovereign 'en force et en volonté; en puissance législative et en puissance exécutive; en droit d'impôts, de justice et de guerre; en administration intérieure, et en pouvoir de traiter avec l'étranger'.[3] The enumeration in itself, comprising a medley of general laws and particular acts, of legislative and executive functions, which corresponds in no way to any logical analysis of the powers of the state, shows that he is not thinking of Montesquieu's broad principle. The danger Rousseau is anxious to ward off is primarily the destruction of the unity of the state by a multiplication of authorities, in the inevitable struggles of which the common interest will vanish.

Rousseau distinguishes and separates the executive, legislative and judicial functions clearly enough. He takes for granted the division of the magistrature between those exercising executive and judicial functions, indicating that the judicial function is to be separated from the legislative because it is concerned with particular acts.[4] In his comments on events in Geneva he argues that to allow the people as such to act as judges in individual cases is to introduce the most flagrant abuse of the wildest democracy.[5] The citizens, he says, will then be no more citizens, but

[1] As e.g. by Mestre, *op. cit.*, p. 466.
[2] Sée, *op. cit.*, p. 150.
[3] *Pol. Writings*, ii. 41 : *Con. soc.*, II. ii.
[4] *id.*, ii. 47 : *Con. soc.*, II. v.
[5] *Corr. Gén.*, xviii. 103 : to Coindet, February 9, 1768.

F

magistrates: 'c'est l'anarchie d'Athènes, et tout est perdu'.[1] He evidently assumes that there is to be a separate class of judges, though preferring the classical idea of choosing these for their general merit from the whole body of citizens, rather than the modern practice of recruiting them exclusively among the class of legal experts. But it is the relationship of the other two members of the trinity of power that constitutes the crux of the question.

We must be careful, in the first place, not to exaggerate the principles of Montesquieu, who does not himself speak of the *séparation*, but of the *partage, division* or *distribution* of powers, and whose object is not so much to isolate as to balance them. Rousseau also gives us, along with an underlying unity, a real separation of powers in the state. The fundamental unity of the state he embodies in the sovereignty of the people; the absolute separation which, unlike Montesquieu, he sets up, is that between the legislative or law-making body, and all those concerned with particular acts; finally, among the various branches of the executive he proposes a *balance* of powers in the true sense of the word, which he calls a *gouvernement mixte*; and as exemplifying this he—like Montesquieu—finds the English Constitution 'un modèle de la juste balance des pouvoirs respectifs'.[2] For the maintenance of the balance in the executive he has recourse to the expedient of the *tribunat*,[3] and though this may seem far-fetched, the point to be stressed is that the separation between the executive government and the sovereign is an essential part of the political system set up in the *Contrat social*; the government is for its author not the sovereign authority, but merely 'un corps intermédiaire établi entre les sujets et le souverain pour leur mutuelle correspondence'.[4]

There is no point in Rousseau's theory which has been so widely misrepresented. Only a complete failure to grasp his basic political principles can explain, for instance, the view that they found their practical embodiment in the Jacobin constitution of 1793. This constitution is often said to exhibit the influence of Rousseau, on the grounds that it established direct government

[1] *id.*, xviii. 114: to d'Ivernois, February 9, 1768.
[2] *Pol. Writings*, ii. 266: Lett. Mont., IX.
[3] *id.*, ii. 118: *Con. soc.*, IV. v.
[4] *id.*, ii. 65; ii. 201.

by the people. In fact it permitted the participation of the people in the task of legislation only in a very attenuated form. Only if those opposed to a law could obtain the support of one-tenth of the primary assemblies in a majority of the *départements* within forty days of the passing of the law, did it have to be referred to a direct vote of the people. As, however, the constitution remained a dead letter and was never put into practice, any discussion of its results must necessarily remain hypothetical.

A more serious argument is presented by Joseph-Barthélemy, who describes the year 1793 as marking the triumph of the *Contrat social*, with the enfeeblement of the notion of individual rights resulting from the omnipotence of the Convention and the preponderance of the legislative power in the Jacobin constitution.[1] But he answers himself when he says elsewhere that the principle of unity of action appears in the Convention as an almost unchallenged dogma.[2] The method by which the Jacobins achieved the unity of direction which France certainly needed, and in fact the essence of their system of government, was indeed the total confusion of the executive with the legislative. Now if by the legislative power we understand the sovereign in Rousseau's sense, we are referring to a body which by definition he allows no share whatsoever in the executive government. According to his theory the legislative power can pass no law unless it be of universal application in the state, and as the government, or executive, is necessarily perpetually concerned with particular acts and decisions, it is by that very fact incapable of possessing sovereign authority. In fact, however, no representative assembly can be sovereign, for the sovereign people as such cannot be represented. Thus neither the Jacobin executive nor the legislative taken separately, still less united, can according to Rousseau be endowed with the slightest shred of rightful sovereignty.

Of course, the constitutional problem of the relations between executive and legislative was understood only to a very limited extent in the eighteenth century. The desirability, for instance, of leaving the power of initiating legislation partly in the hands of the executive, or the wide field of discretion that has to be

[1] J.-Barthélemy, *Le rôle du pouvoir exécutif dans les républiques modernes*, 1906, p. 39.

[2] *id.*, p. 507.

left to the government by even the most carefully framed laws was not appreciated. When he turns to practical politics, in the *Lettres de la Montagne*, Rousseau does not allow the *Conseil général*, the legislative body of Geneva, the right even of initiating the laws for which its approval was necessary.[1] In the same work he treats as particular acts, which therefore are to be left to the discretion of the executive, the forming of alliances with other states, declarations of war and treaties of peace.[2]

One could hardly expect the technique of parliamentary government to be understood at such an early date; experience alone could show what arrangements were and what were not practicable. What one might look for, and what indeed one does find in Rousseau, is a recognition of the importance of leaving to the administration its own proper field of action. This was seen quite clearly at the time and was an argument employed by more than one writer against the revolutionaries. 'Ce qui n'est pas une probabilité, c'est la force avec laquelle Rousseau se fut opposé à ce que l'assemblée nationale se mêlât aucunement de l'administration du royaume; à ce qu'elle s'emparât même provisoirement du pouvoir exécutif et d'une partie du pouvoir judiciaire.'[3] The hostility to the executive in the early years of the revolution, which rapidly died down as the traditions of absolute government reasserted themselves, is not to be attributed to the influence of Rousseau or of Montesquieu. The hatred of the personal government of the Bourbons and the fear of the monarchy are by themselves an adequate explanation. The distinction between executive and legislative may be more difficult to draw in practice than in theory, but so far as he can Rousseau draws it in his practical conclusions as in his theoretical premises.

Rousseau allowed the government or executive only a power of particular action limited by the law. His whole endeavour was to prevent the arrogation of the rights of sovereignty by any governing body whatsoever. He has been misunderstood because his commentators have persistently refused to believe that he meant what he said when he confined the right of sovereignty to the assembly of the whole people. There need not be the

[1] See Vaughan's comments in Pol. Writings, ii. 187.
[2] Pol. Writings, ii. 220: Lett. Mont., VII.
[3] C.-F. Lenormant, J.-J. Rousseau, aristocrate, 1790, pp. 41-2. Cf. Utilitati, L'Assemblée nationale convaincue d'erreur par J.-J. Rousseau, 1792, p. 22.

slightest doubt concerning this, however, for he goes out of his way to prove the practicability of his principle by the examples of the ancient world, the Swiss cantons and Geneva.[1] To anticipate a point that follows, when Bentham scornfully said that no law of any European state would constitute a valid act of sovereignty for Rousseau, except possibly those of the Republic of San Marino, he was saying no more than was true. We need not suppose that Rousseau was blind to such an obvious deduction, even if he had not himself admitted that on a close examination one would find that very few nations have laws.

Although the *Contrat social* is an abstract work in the sense that it is concerned with political principles rather than with the modifications that might be necessary in putting them into practice, certain features which to us may seem clear proof of its impracticable nature had no such implication in the eighteenth century. Indeed Rousseau himself wrote that if he had merely drawn up an abstract system of politics it would have aroused no interest, or at least no serious opposition; his book would have been relegated along with the *Republic* and the *Utopia* 'dans le pays des chimères'. But, he says, he painted the constitution of a state that actually existed, and those who were trying to subvert that constitution naturally could not forgive him.[2] This state was Geneva where, he said,

> Tout petit que j'étois, foible, obscur citoyen,
> Je faisois cependant membre du souverain.[3]

and this fact, even if he exaggerated his debt to his native city, helps us to understand some of the implicit assumptions of the *Contrat social*.[4]

---

[1] *Pol. Writings*, ii. 92-3, 102-3 : *Con. soc.*, III. xii, IV. i.

[2] *id.*, ii. 203 : *Lett. Mont.*, VI.

[3] *Œuvres*, xiii. 418. *Épitre à M. Parisot*, 1742.

[4] That the attempt to attribute Rousseau's political ideas to the influence of the constitution of Geneva was misplaced and misleading was demonstrated by J. S. Spink in *Jean-Jacques et Genève*, 1934. I am not suggesting, of course, that the ideas of any political thinker are to be treated as though they were an abstract construction of the mind, reflecting in a timeless and spaceless void on the products of its own inner consciousness, uncontaminated by acquaintance with the sensual world. On the contrary all true political thinking is historically conditioned and framed toward practical ends. Among the conditions knowledge of which is necessary for its comprehension, not least in importance is its actual political environment. All that is meant here, therefore, is that the practices and problems of Genevan government do not in fact constitute the background of Rousseau's political thinking.

Throughout it is taken for granted by Rousseau that the state, if it is to be a good one, must necessarily be small in extent, confined to a single town and the neighbouring countryside, and approximating in type to the city state. This is not peculiar to him. As has been said, taking Montesquieu, Morelly, Rousseau, Mably, and a host of others, we find that at bottom they uphold one and the same social conception, however widely their other ideals may vary; it is, in the language of d'Argenson, that of a 'ménagerie d'hommes heureux', a little equalitarian republic.[1] Nor does this seem surprising if we reflect that the historical literature of the earlier eighteenth century was still almost exclusively classical. Rousseau himself was an enthusiastic admirer of the classical virtues: the moralist Plutarch was, he claimed, the first reading of his childhood, and would be the last of his old age.[2] In the *Lettre à d'Alembert* he devotes eulogies to Sparta and it is significant that his one attempt at historical writing was a fragment of a history of Lacedaemon. In addition, as has already been pointed out, we have to reckon with the even greater attraction exercised by Geneva over his mind. There is no need to labour the fact of these influences: they are written large throughout his political writings.

Though the influence of education and early environment may count for much in the passion with which Rousseau espouses the cause of the small state, he can support himself also with arguments not lacking in validity. That which goes deepest, to which indeed an answer has hardly yet been found, appears already in the *Discours sur l'inégalité*. 'Si j'avais eu à choisir le lieu de ma naissance, j'aurais choisi une société d'une grandeur bornée par l'étendue des facultés humaines, c'est-à-dire par la possibilité d'être bien gouvernée.[3] Although Rousseau does not proceed to analyse further the desideratum he here indicates, it is quite clear that he has put his finger on one of the fundamental problems of political life. The over-great extension of the modern state and the ill adaptation of human psychology to cope with the huge and complicated nexus of modern society is certainly not less a problem in our time than it was in his.

The conclusions drawn by Rousseau from this argument are to

---

[1] Espinas, *La philosophie sociale du XVIIIe siècle et la Révolution*, 1898, p. 91.
[2] *Confessions, etc.*, iii. 190; *Promeneur solitaire*, IV.
[3] *Pol. Writings*, i. 126.

be found scattered throughout his writings. Those that would have been natural in his own age hardly carry conviction today. He claims, for instance, that in the great state the people will have less affection for leaders whom they never see, a country which is as vast and diverse as a world to them, and for fellow-citizens of whom the great majority must necessarily be strangers.[1] To which we may reply that the remoteness of the leader is not necessarily a disadvantage for him. By allowing him to appear in public only on suitable occasions it facilitates the creation of a public personality which may differ greatly from his real one. For the nation his life can become a series of grand gestures. Thus scope is provided for the development of a legend unhampered by any awareness of defects such as might become evident in the more intimate relationship of a little community. As for the other objection, we need only remark that the patriotic sentiment seems almost limitless in its capacity for expansion.

To come to considerations of possibly a more permanent order, in the small state, says Rousseau, liberty can be greater. The larger the state the stronger the government has to be and the weaker therefore the individual citizen;[2] to which, of course, it might be replied that while his political power may be less, his private freedom may be much more. Again, in the great state the capital inevitably usurps the sovereignty of the nation.[3] Not only is the small state freer, it is also, he believes, stronger in proportion than the large state. 'Plus le lien social s'étend, plus il se relâche.'[4] Its strength, however, is for defence rather than for aggression; its size forbids it to be smitten with the 'féroce amour des conquêtes'.[5] There is, indeed, a maximum size which a state cannot exceed without weakening itself; for the reasons which lead a state to extend its frontiers depend on its external relations, whereas those which tend to keep it in its original limits derive from its nature and internal constitution and are therefore absolute.[6]

[1] *Pol. Writings*, ii. 56-8: *Con. soc.*, II. ix.
[2] *id.*, ii. 154: *Émile*, V.
[3] *id.*, ii. 487: *Con. soc.* (first version).
[4] *id.*, ii. 56: *Con. soc.*, II. ix; *cf. id.* i. 299: *L'état de guerre*.
[5] *id.*, i. 127: *Disc. inég.*
[6] *id.*, ii. 56, 57: *Con. soc.*, II. ix.

The note that Rousseau struck at the beginning of his career is repeated at the end in the *Gouvernement de Pologne*, for the fact that he consented to draft proposals for the reform of the constitution of Poland in no way indicates a change of heart on this question. 'Grandeur des nations, étendue des Etats; première et principale source des malheurs du genre humain, . . . Presque tous les petits Etats . . . prospèrent par cela seul qu'ils sont petits. . . . Tous les grands peuples, écrasés par leurs propres masses, gémissent, ou comme vous dans l'anarchie, ou sous les oppresseurs subalternes qu'une gradation nécessaire force les rois de leur donner.'[1] We must therefore take him quite seriously when in the *Contrat social* he limits his ideal state to a single city and when he complains that he has written only for his native city and similar small states, that he did not dream of reforming the great states of Europe, but only of checking the corruption of those which still retained their original size and something of their primitive simplicity.

We have constantly to keep in mind the distinction between the world for which Rousseau wrote and that in which we read him. When he wrote, as Vaughan reminds us, the development of the nineteenth-century state, with its teeming population and its all-enveloping nationalism could not have been foreseen. Of the complexities of modern industrialism and the continual demand for fresh legislation to meet ever changing circumstances Rousseau had no conception. He is all along thinking of the small, simply organized, conservative state, where the inhabitants live as their fathers have lived, and where, once the constitution has been established, the passing of new laws would be a very rare event.[2] This is worth bearing in mind, because the legislative sovereignty of the state would thus only occasionally be called into force; in the main it would be concerned simply with safeguarding the constitution; and practically everything that we would normally characterize as activities of government would be left to the executive, the authority of which was strictly limited. The consequence to the liberty of the individual of an attempt to subject the great state of today to a political system conceived for Corsica or Andorra would be incalculable

[1] *id.*, ii. 442: *Gouv. Pol.*
[2] *e.g. id.*, ii. 239, 265: *Lett. Mont.*, VIII. ix.

and possibly disastrous, but Rousseau never envisaged any such possibility.

When he condemned the representative system, then, Rousseau certainly did not fail to observe the difficulties in the way of the exercise of sovereignty by the community as a whole in any large state; and if he refused to allow its delegation to any other body it was because the fear of tyranny was greater in his mind than the desire to erect a system practicable in the great states of his day. As one commentator puts it, when Rousseau refuses to allow the general will to be repreesnted, in effect he says, 'I do not allow to any existing institution sufficient social morality to be the interpreter of my needs and the defender of my interests; I believe it invincibly inclined to misuse in its own interests the power that I give it'.[1] We may think that Rousseau is unduly fearful of the 'unending audacity of elected persons', but at least his caution serves to demonstrate—and this is the point of relevance here—the importance he attaches to the distinction between the legislative and the executive powers.

Yet the confusion of the two is frequent in critics of Rousseau. Thus one, after quoting the passage in which he maintains that only the sovereign can judge what matters concern the whole community, goes on to remark, 'Ce qui rend l'administration tracassière, intolerante, tyrannique . . . ce n'est pas autre chose que l'opinion qu'elle se fait de l'utilité publique, qu'elle interprète, du reste, à sa façon'[2]—a very just observation in itself but one which reads *administration* where Rousseau had written *sovereign*. Another writer explains that the exercise of the legislative power by the people is according to Rousseau one of the traits of democracy, a government which he admits to be suitable only for a people of gods.[3] On the contrary, of course, according to Rousseau the exercise of the legislative power by the people is the sign of every legitimate state, whatever the form of government, and the system which he condemns as altogether impracticable for men is democracy in the strict sense of the term, the exercise not of the legislative but of the executive power by the whole people.

[1] Tchernoff, 'Montesquieu et J.-J. Rousseau', *Revue du droit public*, 1903, xix. 477-514; xx. 49-97, 506.

[2] H. Rodet, '*Le contrat social*' *et les idées politiques de J.-J. Rousseau*, 1909, pp. 96-7.

[3] Tchernoff, *op. cit.*, p. 501.

The misunderstanding is even more strikingly evident in a passage by Duguit, where one can see that the writer in passing from one sentence to another unconsciously substitutes the term government for sovereignty, and thus entirely falsifies the theory of Rousseau. 'La constitution de 1793, sans le dire expressément,' he says, 'avait écarté l'idée de la représentation; ses auteurs, s'inspirant surtout de J.-J. Rousseau, étaient dominés par l'idée que la souveraineté ne peut pas plus être representée qu'elle ne peut être alienée. A cause de cela, ils avaient fait une large part au gouvernement direct.'[1] Leaving on one side the actual fact that the constitution of 1793 did not reject the principle of representation, and that the government of the Jacobins was much nearer to dictatorship than to the direct government of the people, it is only necessary to remind ourselves that Rousseau anyhow specifically rules out direct government, which in his, as in classical terminology, is the interpretation of democracy. 'Vous avez pu voir,' he writes to d'Ivernois, 'dans le *Contrat social* que je n'ai jamais approuvé le gouvernement Démocratique.'[2] It is true, he admits, that by putting the executive power as well as the legislative in the hands of the people, democracy averts the creation of a separate *volonté de corps* attached to the government, but also it calls, he thinks, for superhuman virtues. It is for this reason, he believes, that no true democracy has ever existed or ever will exist. It is a form of government fit for gods, not for men,[3] for whom, indeed, the system in which the wills of the government and of the legislative are most distinct—elective aristocracy, which we would call parliamentary government, is the best.[4]

It may be urged, finally, that Rousseau in the *Lettres de la Montagne* allows the sovereign a right of general superintendence over the executive. He says that once every twenty years or so the sovereign must meet to consider both the constitution and the way in which it has been observed by the government, from which it has been concluded that he abandons Montesquieu's theory of the separation of powers. Barthélemy,[5] who

---

[1] L. Duguit, *Traité de Droit Constitutionnel*, 2nd ed., 1923, ii. 18.
[2] *Corr. Gén.*, xvi. 229: to d'Ivernois, January 31, 1767.
[3] *Pol. Writings*, ii. 74: *Con. soc.*, III. iv.
[4] *id.*, ii. 75: *Con. soc.*, III. v; *cf. id.*, ii. 202.
[5] Barthélemy, *op. cit.*, pp. 420-2.

raises this specific point, has himself shown, however, that Rousseau is here merely following Montesquieu, when he claims that in a free state the legislative power should have the right of examining the way in which the laws it has passed are executed.[1] As for the actual government, Rousseau always insists that it must be in the hands of the magistrates alone, and that these must be free from any interference by the legislative power.[2] Though the people have the right of sovereignty, they are not competent according to him to control the details of government, the constitution and the conduct of which he leaves to the executive, as matters of convenience, to be settled according to the circumstances of the state.[3]

While he thus allows the sovereign a certain strictly limited right of supervision over the executive, the latter is allowed no corresponding rights in return. If there is one idea to be found running through all Rousseau's political writings it is that the sovereign makes the law and that it is the mark of all legitimate government to be under the law. To give only two of many quotations we might make to illustrate this principle, in the *Lettres de la Montagne* he declares, 'Un peuple est libre, quelque forme qu'ait son Gouvernement, quand, dans celui qui le gouverne, il ne voit point l'homme, mais l'organe de la Loi'.[4] This he holds true whether the state be monarchy or democracy: 'La puissance exécutive n'est que la force; et où règne la seule force, l'Etat est dissous. Voilà, monsieur, comment pèrissent à la fin tous les Etats démocratiques.'[5] We may remind ourselves that the principle of the *ancien régime* was precisely the reverse of Rousseau's, for its authority was always personal and based in the last resort on the absolute will of the king.

4. ROUSSEAU AND THE DEMOCRATIC STATE

In the light of what has been said above we can now turn to a consideration of the relevance of Rousseau's ideas to the modern

---

[1] *Esprit des Lois*, bk. XI, ch. VI. 'Elle (the legislative power) a droit et doit avoir la faculté d'examiner de quelle manière les loix qu'elle a faites ont été exécutées.' He adds that ministers who have not kept the laws may be sought out and punished.

[2] *Pol. Writings*, i. 128: *Disc. inég.*

[3] *id.*, ii. 186.

[4] *id.*, ii. 235: *Lett. Mont.*, VIII; *cf. id.*, i. 126, 245; ii. 426-7.

[5] *id.*, ii. 209: *Lett. Mont.*, VII.

democratic state. The essential difference between Rousseau and most of the writers who upheld these ideas in the ninetcenth century is that he does not assume any automatic connection between the two principles of individual and social welfare. He does not admit that the personal, selfish interest of the individual is necessarily allied to the well-being of the community. On the contrary, he says, 'Ils s'excluent l'un l'autre dans l'ordre naturel des choses'.[1] Now the utilitarian argument for democracy, in its simplest form, is based on this identification, although in fact utilitarianism is not logically incompatible with despotism. The individual may be tyrannized over for his own benefit, and it is on this ground that most despotic governments of the modern world have been defended. Individualism, on the other hand, can give us no satisfactory reason by itself why any individual should consider the welfare of the community. On these lines the theoretic justification for the modern democratic state is certainly weak. To what extent is Rousseau with his theory of the general will more successful?

The interpretation of Rousseau as an ancestor of the modern system of democratic ideas has never been seriously challenged, and this in spite of the numerous aspects on which his theory is in open contradiction with the basic conditions of modern democratic society. These are so obvious that they hardly need to be repeated—his hostility to the representative principle and to the great state, his preference for local autonomy, dislike for large cities and a highly developed and artificial social life, for frequent legislative changes—one might almost say that he condemns in advance practically all the characteristic features of democracy. For what reasons, then, can we regard Rousseau as a precursor of democracy? The answer sometimes given is that he changed the emphasis from reason to emotion in the analysis of man as a political animal. For most ancient and modern philosophers the peculiar character of man and his highest faculty is the reason, which however is admitted to be the dominant power in but few. The majority, the masses, are moved only by self-interest and passion. Therefore, it is argued, the rule of reason implies the sovereignty of the few, if not of one, in other words of an aristocracy or of a philosopher king. In Rousseau's thought, it is alleged, the process is reversed and for reason are substituted

[1] id., i. 450: Con. soc. (first version).

instinct and sentiment as the ruling faculties and chief guide in politics. Now instinct and sentiment have a greater power over the people than over those who reason. Therefore, the argument concludes, he gives sovereignty to the people.[1]

In this interpretation of Rousseau there is an element of truth, for he does not regard reasoning as providing by itself a sure foundation for political society; and certainly in his ideal state the legislative power is in the hands of the people and not the possession of one man or a small ruling class. What I would question is the assumption that the one is a deduction drawn from the other and that the result is equivalent to the rule of unreason.

Rousseau criticized the intellectualist psychology which attributed all action to conscious motivation, and from this the prevalent view of him as an enemy of reason largely springs. The influence of Cartesian rationalism is however writ large in his works, and if he allows the emotions a great part in his political system, that is to be attributed to his keener sense of political realities. After all, as Hume said, man is moved primarily by his passions; it is no great virtue in a student of politics to pretend otherwise, to ignore the passions, instead of attempting to organize and master them. But though Rousseau has no blind faith in the intellect as a political force, his theory is altogether on the side of reason if we compare it with that which came after and in the name of emotion, sentiment, tradition, upheld the aristocratic and monarchical system of the past against the new, Rousseauist, democratic ideas.

His belief in the people as the legislative power is based not on irrational sentiment but on the conviction that the people as a whole forms the only power in the state which is not interested in perverting it to selfish and sectional ends. 'L'intérêt personnel,' he says, 'augmente à mesure que l'association devient plus étroite . . . preuve invincible que la volonté la plus génèrale est aussi toujours la plus juste.'[2] Acton, in a manuscript note, sums up Rousseau's argument so clearly that we cannot do better than quote him. 'The constant and spontaneous sentiment of the masses, on matters which concern them all, is sure to be right—

[1] cf. *Bulletin de la société française de philosophie*, vii, December 27, 1906, pp. 69-70.

[2] *Pol. Writings*, i. 243 : *Écon. pol.*

Masses judge not by theories, but by facts—It is the mass as opposed to the individual — The individual is presumably interested, narrow, selfish, swayed by theories—Private interest instead of general interest.'[1]

Rousseau thus attributes the qualities of social utility and justice to the unperverted will of the people. 'Souvent,' he says in the *Lettres de la Montagne*, 'l'injustice et la fraude trouvent des protecteurs; jamais elles n'ont le public pour elles: c'est en ceci que la voix du peuple est la voix de Dieu.'[2] Truly a dangerous statement, and one which takes us far into the deepest meaning of the general will and seems to make it the final arbiter of right and wrong. Rousseau's unequivocal rejection of all elements of revelation, grace and the supernatural in religion, and the opposition introduced in modern times between religion and reason, have tended to obscure the mystical element in his thought, but its recognition is essential for understanding it. With this in mind, indeed, we can see the conception of the general will in a different light. C. W. Hendel many years ago put forward a suggestion that has not been sufficiently followed up.[3] The idea of the general will, he pointed out, was not invented by Rousseau, who met it in Malebranche, both directly and through the writings of Father Lamy, though it must have looked very different there, for it was not the general will of the state, but the general will of God. Here, it may be suggested, is the source of that terrestrial general will which is the embodiment of perfect goodness on earth, in which, as Rousseau sets forth in the first paragraph of the *Contrat social*, right is united with interest, and justice with utility.

This is not equivalent to saying that the general will is irrational. Even if he believes that it can be discovered from the naturally good sentiments of the many rather than the selfish enlightenment of the few, the idea of the general will is still a rational ideal. As he put it in the first version of the *Contrat social*, the exercise of sovereignty, or the general will, is 'dans chaque individu un acte pur de l'entendement qui raisonne dans le silence des passions sur ce que l'homme peut exiger de son semblable, et sur ce que son semblable est en droit d'exiger de

---

[1] Acton MSS., Cambridge Univ. Lib., Add. 5409.

[2] Pol. *Writings*, ii. 256: *Lett. Mont.*, VIII.

[3] C. W. Hendel, *Jean-Jacques Rousseau, Moralist*, 1934, i. 119-20.

lui'.[1] It is not necessarily identifiable with any actual will. For suppose, says Rousseau, the state is wholly corrupt, and all its members, ruled by their own private motives, enact falsely under the name of laws iniquitous decrees directed only to their own selfish interests, does it follow that the general will is destroyed or corrupted? No, he answers—and it is here that the true nature of the general will appears—'*elle est toujours constante, inaltérable et pure*'.[2] In other words, it is an ideal: it is what the will of the community would be if it were free from distortion by particular interests, and perfect in its enlightenment and goodness. It is not heard in the howls of Metternich's mob, beating at his gates. Rousseau would distinguish as strictly as Burke himself between the passions of the populace and the voice of a people judging deliberately, in accordance with the light of reason, and under right guidance, on its own proper and permanent interests.[3]

Yet Rousseau was a son of the people: he put his trust in the people as he did in no governing classes. In the last analysis there is, one must confess, a certain emotional colouring in his theory. One might argue that what he is doing is deepening and expanding, in fact giving a real content, to *vertu*, the character according to Montesquieu necessary to the people under a republican polity. Rousseau was theorizing before the event, groping in the darkness towards a new idea of the state, and one about which— in spite of his love of the ancients—he could really gain very little information from the classics. Looking back, we may say that his theory is an attempt to describe what we would call government by enlightened public opinion; but inevitably his anticipations, however intelligent, lack the reality that is only to be gained by concrete experience. Not what he himself would have said, but the language in which a philosopher with more knowledge of the operation of an at any rate partially democratic society would express a parallel idea, is to be found in Green: 'If the sovereign power is to be understood in this fuller, less abstract sense, if we mean by it the real determinant of the habitual obedience of the people, . . . it can no longer be said to reside in a determinate person or persons, but in that

[1] *Pol. Writings*, i. 452: *Con. soc.* (first version).
[2] id., ii. 103: *Con. soc.*, IV. i.
[3] id., ii. 256: *Lett. Mont.*, VIII.

impalpable congeries of the hopes and fears of a people, bound together by common interests and sympathy, which we call the general will'.[1]

Up to a point this is equivalent to government by public opinion, and in a manner of speaking, of course, public opinion is always the determining factor in the state. But the illustrations usually given of the weakness of despotism when opposed by public opinion are proof of no more than a negative power, a capacity for resistance. The Sultan, it used to be said, could not compel his subjects to change their headgear. Where the old traditional authorities were incapable of effecting changes, for the very reason that they were themselves based on the absence of change erected into a principle, newer dictatorial rulers, strong in an embodiment, even if only a temporary one, of the national will, have proved irresistible. The novelty in Rousseau's argument is that he attributes to the people not merely a power of veto, which has been generally recognized, and which can also be a way of expressing the tyranny of custom or tradition, he gives them also positive charge of their own destinies. Nor will he allow any limitation to the power of the general will, any fundamental law which it is obliged to accept; not even the terms of the social contract itself are sacred.[2] It is worth pointing out that one system of government in which this unlimited legislative supremacy—though of a representative body and not of the people as such—is accepted in theory and in practice is the English parliamentary democracy: even in Geneva the principle of a fundamental law was an integral part of the constitution.

A further consequence of Rousseau's principles is the abandonment of the idea that the laws are the expression of divine ordinance. Thus he comes into conflict both with the theorists of divine right, and with the later theocratic school, for whom all human legislation was declaratory of divine justice. It was natural that to writers such as de Maistre the theory of Rousseau should seem the most impious arrogation of power and the very embodiment of tyranny. For he excludes the possibility of attributing sovereignty to any person or body other than the whole people, while the will of the people itself is only sovereign when

[1] Green, op. cit., § 86; Works, ii. 404.
[2] Pol. Writings, ii. 34-5: Con. soc., I. vii; cf. id., ii. 468: Gouv. Pol.

it embodies the general will. But to the general will he allows the most extensive powers as the one and only source of law.

The result, in church and state, is truly revolutionary. The traditional and hereditary rights of priest, noble or king disappear at a blow. The idea of the sovereignty of the people is necessarily fatal to the regime of authority in both ecclesiastical and civil spheres. Monarchical divine right, legacy of the Middle Ages, and aristocratic privileges, the last bulwark of feudal law, both receive the final challenge. Rousseau's predecessor, Locke, although in implication no less formidable to the existing order of things, does not seem so drastic because he provides us with an apparent compromise. By acknowledging the human origin of the laws Rousseau automatically puts society in charge of its own destiny, and in this sense it was really he, rather than Voltaire, who restored to the human race its titles. This does not mean that he frees political power from all restraint; but the limits he recognizes are those imposed by human nature itself, by the human ethical conscience, and by the positive circumstances of the state.

The *ancien régime*, the old semi-theocratic, semi-feudal, monarchical state, completely loses, with Rousseau, its intellectual justification. The newer irreligious and utilitarian despotism, called benevolent, equally goes by the board. And what is left, his critics would say, is the rule of the people—controlled by no conception of a superior law, moderated by no divided sources of right or authority, trammelled by no respect for tradition, veiled by no religious awe—the simple, stark, naked absolutism of the general will. The extent to which this judgment requires to be modified I have already indicated. As concerns the political machinery of the state and the relation of the individual to the government it is obviously false. Yet it contains in the last resort a certain truth. Public opinion may be the force limiting all despotisms, but in the modern state what is it that shall limit the tyranny of public opinion? Theoretically, Rousseau may have surrounded it with all the safeguards posited in the definition of the general will; but was it not to be feared that the idea might be seized on and the safeguards forgotten? And, his philosophical arguments neglected, were there not grounds for fearing that the dominance of the popular will, of the mass mind, might be a more serious menace to individual freedom than the

G

power of any king? Rousseau, it is true, is hardly justly to be blamed for developments he could never have anticipated, which would have filled him with revulsion. Yet in one respect, indeed, there is an embryo absolutism in his political gospel itself, but it is of a new kind and not to be understood until we have studied another aspect of his theory; for the sovereignty of the general will came in practice, and even to some extent in his thought, to mean that newer form of political absolutism which we call nationalism.

CHAPTER IV

ROUSSEAU AND THE NATION STATE

1. REVOLT AGAINST THE COSMOPOLITAN IDEAL

Political theory, even at its most metaphysical, can never be entirely divorced from practical politics, and Rousseau's was much closer to realities than his critics are generally willing to allow. Indeed I would be more disposed to charge him with an undue tendency to justify facts than with totally disregarding them, if it were not that by itself the distinction is a vain one. The very *raison d'être* of political theory is to find which political facts to justify and which to condemn, and the latter process, if not equivalent to total disregard, is an equally drastic denial of validity. The real issue is which particular sets of facts to accept, and which to reject. Rousseau was regarded as a dreamer because the facts from which he derived his political ideas were different from the facts as most of his contemporaries saw them. For most thinkers of the eighteenth century the subject matter of discussion in politics was provided by the states of the contemporary world as revealed in a rather narrowly political interpretation of their history, together with such material as could be obtained from a superficial knowledge of the classics, which omitted from its ken all of what one might call the more platonic elements in the life of the city state. The only political relation recognized, the link binding the individual members of the state together, was the relation of government and subject. The basic political idea was therefore that of legal sovereignty.

With Rousseau, however, it is not enough to examine his political views merely in connection with that agglomeration of territory, united by its subjection to a single ruler, which constituted the characteristic state of the eighteenth century. His discussion even of the theory of sovereignty itself leads him, as we have seen, far from the beaten track of eighteenth-century political thought. In this chapter I hope to show that he was conscious of the coming of a new type of state based on national sentiment.

Such nations as were already states, even France itself, had still to be born to self-consciousness out of the agony of the revolutionary and Napoleonic Wars. For the appearance of the nation state no political inventor can be given the credit or blame, and it is not my intention to saddle Rousseau with either. But the fact that he is perhaps its first theorist is undeniable. Not only is his theory of the general will applicable to the nation state of the future whereas it is obviously without relevance to the absolutist state of his own time, but he brings the national idea definitely into operation in connection with two of the few practical manifestations of national spirit that troubled the even path of eighteenth-century despotism. Nevertheless it is an aspect of his political thinking which, although adumbrated in general terms by one or two commentators, has been given practically no detailed examination. Yet without this one cannot help feeling that it is almost impossible to appreciate his place in the history of political thought or to grasp as a whole his ideas on the nature and functions of the state.[1]

The novelty of the national idea at the end of the eighteenth century is generally admitted, though the attitude of individual citizens towards the states of which they were members is not a subject on which it is easy to generalize. It varied from the jingoism of *Rule Britannia* to the cosmopolitanism affected by the *philosophes*, from the blind obedience of Prussians to the anarchical independence of Polish nobles. In England the patriotic appeal could always raise the enthusiasm of the mob; in the petty German and Italian states patriotism can hardly have existed at all. Nowhere were the masses politically conscious or articulate. The absence of popular resistance to the

---

[1] Apart from Vaughan, when this book was first written I had found only three such references. Höffding speaks incidentally of Rousseau's great service in provoking a renaissance of patriotic feeling at the time when political life was petrified in obsolete forms. Professor Holland Rose says that the national idea is fundamental to the *Contrat social*, though he does not attempt to develop this view. While Professor Irving Babbitt in a passing reference adds nationalism to the already long catalogue of modern iniquities which he lays to the charge of Rousseau. Vaughan is the only writer to give this aspect of Rousseau's political thinking anything more than a brief reference, and while he emphasizes the fact that the *Gouvernement de Pologne* marks the triumph of the national idea in Rousseau's mind, and compares with this the conversion of Wordsworth a generation later, he seems hardly to realize the full significance of the idea and dismisses it very briefly. (Vaughan, *Political Writings of Rousseau*, ii. 389-90.)

revolutionary armies of France, except in Spain, is eloquent of the real condition of the feelings of the people. Genuine national sentiments are perhaps only to be seen among those middle classes whose economic interests were closely bound up with colonial expansion. The *noblesse* in France, as the revolution showed, were loyal rather to their order than to their country; in fact one might say, with Chateaubriand, that for them national feelings were only born out of the nostalgia of exile, 'ce mélange de tendresse et de mélancolie, qu'on nomme *l'amour de son pays*'.[1] Finally, to give no more illustrations, when we find Irish Catholics fighting on the side of France against French Huguenot regiments in the English army, it is obvious that religion was still a rival claiming often deeper allegiance than the state.

There was doubtless much latent patriotic feeling in many countries, and one must be careful not to mistake the affectations of a literary clique for the sentiments of a people; nevertheless literature was in the eighteenth century very closely connected with the world of affairs and in the matter of patriotism reflects not unfaithfully current opinion. In eighteenth-century France the predominant tendency in literature was that of the *philosophes*, who prided themselves on their freedom from patriotic prejudices. Not that, as is sometimes supposed, they despised the patriotic ideal itself. But, as Montesquieu said, writing of monarchical government and not without reference to his own day, 'L'état subsiste indépendamment de l'amour pour la patrie, du désir de la vraie gloire, du renoncement à soi-même, du sacrifice de ses plus chers intérêts, et de toutes ces vertus héroïques que nous trouvons dans les anciens, et dont nous avons seulement entendu parler'.[2] He means to imply that patriotism is too noble an emotion, too republican a virtue, to be found in modern times. It is to Montesquieu that we can look for the source, in the eighteenth century, of the doctrine that patriotism is incompatible with despotic government, for by making *vertu*, defined as 'l'amour des lois et de la patrie',[3] the political motive exclusive to republics, he links this political sentiment, which is

---

[1] Chateaubriand, *Œuvres* (Garnier Frères, s.d.), i. 296: *Essai sur les Révolutions*, 1796.

[2] *Esprit des Lois*, bk. III, ch. V.

[3] *id.*, bk. III, ch. III; bk. IV, ch. V.

closely akin to what we would call patriotism, with free government. The Chevalier de Jaucourt in the *Encyclopédie* draws the
conclusion that, 'Ceux qui vivent sous le despotisme oriental, où
on ne connoît d'autre loi que la volonté du souverain, . . . n'ont
point de *patrie*'.[1]

The explanation the *philosophes* offered for the absence of
patriotic spirit was inadequate: ample evidence exists to prove
that there is nothing essentially incompatible between patriotism
and despotic government. The true cause lies in the fundamental
difference between the ancient and the modern state. It is almost
impossible for the citizen of the modern state — and more
especially was this true in the eighteenth century—to feel himself identified in his every activity with the state in the way of
the ancient world. Moreover it followed from their classical
studies that when they did think of patriotism the *philosophes*
conceived it as essentially connected with the relation of the
individual to the sovereign body called the state. The eighteenth
century was largely oblivious to the political potentialities
of that other bond connecting men in society, the sense of
nationality. This is not necessarily identified with statehood, the
essential distinction between patriotism and the spirit of
nationality being that the one is an emotion aroused by the idea
of the state, and the other by the idea of the nation. But
eighteenth-century usage did not distinguish between nation and
state. The *Encyclopédie* defines *nation* as, 'Mot collectif dont on
fait usage pour exprimer une quantité considérable de peuple,
qui habite une certaine étendue de pays, renfermée dans de certaines limites, et qui obéit au même gouvernement'.[2]

In the eighteenth century, while most of the *philosophes*
admired the classical spirit of patriotism, they disliked national
differences, ignored the existence of nationality as an historical
force, and if they had been aware of any general claim to national
independence would certainly have repudiated a right based on
nothing more rational than sentiment and tradition. That is the
truth behind Rousseau's rather sweeping condemnation: 'La
famille, la patrie deviennent pour lui des mots vides de sens: il
n'est ni parent, ni citoyen, ni homme; il est philosophe'.[3]

[1] *Encyclopédie*, art. 'Patrie'.
[2] *Encyclopédie*, art. 'Nation'.
[3] *Œuvres*, viii. xviii: Preface to *Narcisse*.

Although medieval anticipations may be found, conscious nationalism first became a force in world history during the nineteenth century. The classical idea of patriotism, the only kind known to the eighteenth century, by the end of the revolutionary period had been extensively supplanted by the idea of loyalty to the nation. The importance of the revolutionary period in this transformation is obvious: Why at this time the national idea should have commenced its career of world-wide conquest is a question almost impossible to answer, unless we say, as Hegel said of another explosive force, that the world had need of it and therefore it appeared; and indeed the role of nationalism in the political evolution of Europe and the world renders it not unworthy of the philosophical praise once awarded to gunpowder. However, though one cannot speak of nationality as a general political force before the revolutionary period, the idea certainly appears before the revolution.[1] In the incidental observations of Burke on the suppression of the Corsicans by French troops and on the First Partition of Poland, the right of national independence is definitely recognized. It was precisely these events which provided Rousseau with the occasion for what one may fairly term a more comprehensive and a more clearly expounded theory of nationality than that of Burke.

He begins with a conception of patriotism not far removed from that of the *philosophes*. Prepared by his Genevan environment to appreciate some of the characteristic features of the life of the city state, he never really emancipated himself from classical ideals in politics, and as late as the *Gouvernement de Pologne* we find him drawing melancholy comparisons between the patriotism elicited by ancient political institutions and the vicious cosmopolitanism of his own day.[2] '*L'institution publique*', in the proper sense of the word, cannot exist in the absence of patriotism; since where there is no *patrie* there can be no possibility of citizenship.[3] He does not say that where there is no freedom there can be no patriotism; instead he reverses the accepted maxim, and declares that where there is no *patrie* there can be no freedom. Although with this significant change of emphasis, Rousseau, like Montesquieu, connects patriotism with

[1] Cobban, *op. cit.*, ch. IV.
[2] Pol. *Writings*, ii. 429-30.
[3] *id.*, ii. 146: *Émile.*

republican virtue—'La patrie ne peut subsister sans la liberté, ni la liberté sans la vertu, ni la vertu sans les citoyens'.[1]

But Rousseau does not stop at this. In him we can see plainly the transition from the classical ideal of patriotism to the modern ideal of nationality. He exalts the patriotic spirit, as did the *philosophes*, but instead of an historical tradition or a literary pose, it becomes for him something more vital. He imports it into a new world of thought, and so doing changes it and intensifies its significance. His theory of the contract fits consistently enough into the development of traditional political ideas; his originality lies in that conception of the general will which leads him irresistibly towards the idea of nationality. Here he stands alone, for the only other pre-revolutionary political writer to see the oncoming of the age of nationality was his greatest critic, Edmund Burke.

For both Burke and Rousseau the idea of nationality springs out of their newer attitude towards political society, though the eloquence of Burke's description of the life of society far transcends that of Rousseau. They both realize that the bases of political life and men's motives in society are more often emotional than intellectual. There is in Rousseau a contradiction between the author of the *Contrat social*, whose political psychology is on the whole rationalist, and the commentator on contemporary political facts. In the latter role one can trace an increasing consciousness of the irrational, beginning in the Second Discourse with a recognition of the motive force of passion, for which Rousseau may be indebted to Diderot.[2] In the *Economie politique* he applies the idea to the political sphere, maintaining that a man without passions would make an extremely bad citizen.[3] Replying to an intellectualist utilitarianism, the *Lettre à Mirabeau* of 1767 asks of whom we can say that his conduct is dictated by his real interests, and answers, 'Le sage seul, s'il existe'.[4] Where are there men, he demands, who follow even their own maxims? Reason shows us the end, the passions lead us away from it.[5] The essence of society consisting in the

---

[1] id., i. 255: Écon. pol.
[2] id., i. 150; cf. id., i. 120.
[3] id., i. 255.
[4] id., ii. 160; cf. id., ii. 168.
[5] Œuvres, viii. ix: Preface to *Narcisse*.

activity of its members, the state itself can be no more free from passion than the individuals of which it is comprised. This is his answer, he says, to the many writers who have dared to declare, 'que le Corps politique est sans passions, et qu'il n'y a point d'autre raison d'Etat que la raison même'.[1] It forms an argument, incidentally, of considerable efficacy against the Idealists, whom some have accounted his disciples.

The *Corsica*, and still more the *Poland*, represent the practical application of his new view of political life. In Corsica, he congratulated himself, he had been the first to see a nation capable of discipline and freedom where others had seen only a band of brigands. 'Je vis germer les palmes de cette nation naissante,' he writes. The French conquest, shocking to 'toute justice, toute humanité, toute politique, toute raison', shattered for ever his hopes and the prospects of Corsican independence;[2] but the ultimate success of France in such an unequal struggle was hardly proof of Rousseau's impracticability. He saw only too clearly how difficult it was for the small state to survive in a world of warring imperialisms. In Poland, again, the national spirit was to have a long history of struggle with adversity. In the case of Poland, also, and here with ultimate though long delayed justification, he develops the belief, implicit in the theory of the general will, that the will of the people is the ultimate basis of the state. We must not exaggerate the contrast between these essays in the realm of practical politics and the more theoretical *Contrat social*, for the same idea is implied in a passage of that work. 'A ces trois sortes de lois il s'en joint une quatrième, qui ne se grave ni sur le marbre, ni sur l'airain, mais dans les cœurs des citoyens; qui fait la véritable constitution de l'Etat; qui prend tous les jours de nouvelles forces; qui, lorsque les autres lois vieillissent, ou s'éteignent, les ranime ou les supplée, conserve un peuple dans l'esprit de son institution, et substitue insensiblement la force de l'habitude à celle de l'autorité. Je parle des mœurs, des coutumes, et surtout de l'opinion.'[3] In any case, the result of combining a belief in the power of public opinion with a realization of its emotional nature is to provide scope for an appreciation of elements in political life which the intellectualist

[1] *Pol. Writings*, i. 298: *L'état de guerre*; cf. *id.*, i. 365.
[2] *Corr. Gén.*, xix. 257 n.: to Saint-Germain, February 26, 1770.
[3] *Pol. Writings*, ii. 63-4: *Con. soc.*, II. xii; cf. *id.*, i. 322: *Fragments*.

theories disregarded—and of these the greatest was the force of nationality.

We are now perhaps in a better position to understand Rousseau's crusade against the cosmopolitan tendencies of his age, and why he should have set himself up against what we cannot but regard as one of the humaner and more generous ideals of the century. While still under the influence of the philosophical sect with which he associated when he first went to Paris, he wrote in praise of 'quelques grandes âmes cosmopolites, qui franchissent les barrières imaginaires qui séparent les peuples, et qui, à l'exemple de l'Etre souverain qui les a créés, embrassent tout le genre humain dans leur bienveillance'.[1] The natural tendencies of his mind are shown, however, even in the First Discourse, where he attacks those who despise the old phrases, religion and *patrie*, and devote their talents to the destruction of what is most sacred to mankind. After he had quarrelled with the Encyclopaedists, he was perhaps for that very reason all the bitterer against those whom he now called pretended cosmopolitans, who boasted of their love for humanity in order to have the right to hate their neighbours.[2] In the well-known passage of the *Emile* in which he scornfully says, 'Tel Philosophe aime les Tartares, pour être dispensé d'aimer ses voisins',[3] was he not thinking of the enthusiasm of Voltaire and Diderot for the Empress Catherine or of literature in general for the realm of Kubla Khan?

While the attack on cosmopolitanism was part of his general campaign against the *philosophes*, it also had a less personal basis, in an argument which appears before his final breach with them. As early as the *Economie politique* he had explained that the sentiment of humanity becomes weaker by being extended to the whole world. This sentiment, he says, can only be useful to those with whom we are brought into immediate contact; it becomes the stronger by being confined to our fellow-citizens, and the greatest triumphs of *vertu* have been the product of national sentiment.[4] Such are to be expected no longer. Cosmopolitanism has destroyed the roots of patriotic ardour. In this as

[1] *Pol. Writings*, i. 182: *Disc. inég.*
[2] id., i. 453: *Con. soc.* (first version); cf. id., i. 449-50.
[3] *Œuvres*, i. 9: *Émile*, I; cf. *Pol. Writings*, ii. 145.
[4] *Pol. Writings*, i. 251.

in practically every other respect Rousseau's outlook on his own age is that of a complete pessimist. In the *Gouvernement de Pologne* is his despairing cry, 'Il n'y a plus aujourd'hui de Français, d'Allemands, d'Espagnols, d'Anglais même, quoi qu'on en dise; il n'y a que des Européens'.[1]

Almost endless exordiums to patriotic virtue are to be found in his works. Himself a proudly patriotic Genevan, he might have used on his own behalf the words he puts into the mouth of Claire d'Orme, 'Plus je contemple ce petit Etat, plus je trouve qu'il est beau d'avoir une patrie'.[2] 'L'amour de la patrie,' he says, speaking here for himself, is, 'plus vif et plus délicieux cent fois que celui d'une maîtresse.'[3] And though the decree against his works issued by the magistrates of Geneva provoked him to declare that he had cut his former patriotic sentiments towards his city from out of his heart, in the end he was compelled to confess that he had not been able to detach his affections from his city and that nothing in the world could do so.[4] But he does not stop at this; it is when he develops and applies the ideal of the nation that the originality of Rousseau appears most clearly. His insight is shown not so much by the negative undermining of a somewhat baseless cosmopolitanism, which while of little practical effect, did at least represent the re-birth of the œcumenical idea, as by the positive ideals that he put in its place.

2. THE DEFINITION OF A NATION

Rousseau's theory of nationality is based on an assertion of the reality of what the *philosophes* regarded as the 'artificial' distinctions between nations. Even the abstract *Contrat social* begins essentially at this point. He denies roundly that the despotic state can have a public weal or form a *corps politique*. Such an agglomeration, held together by mere force, does not interest him. The question he presents to himself is in what manner a people becomes such.[5] His object in this work is not to discover what a nation is, but how a body of individuals becomes

---

[1] *id.*, ii. 432.
[2] *Nouv. Hél.*, iv. 205.
[3] *Pol. Writings*, i. 251: *Écon. pol.*
[4] *Corr. Gén.*, xviii. 177: to d'Ivernois, March 24, 1768.
[5] *Pol. Writings*, ii. 31: *Con. soc.*, I. v.

a state, how, that is, rightful political authority is born. In answer to this question he introduces the idea of the general will, and this in fact provides a certain justification for commencing here a study of Rousseau's conception of the nation; for it will not be difficult to show that the theory of the general will is closely bound up with the modern idea of nationality, in the development of which it plays an essential part.

The wilder nineteenth-century theories of a corporate consciousness or a national soul represent, in a sense, developments of the national principle, but the violent manifestations that are apt to result from these perversions are no more proof of a healthy activity than fever is of the proper functioning of the human body. But without having recourse to such extreme doctrines, some more intimate relationship between the members of society than was provided by eighteenth-century individualism, some idea of the moral personality of a state or a community, as something different from the individual wills of its ruler or rulers, was required before the idea of the nation could have any reality. The general will provided this, not only in itself, but also by what it implied—the existence of a certain body of traditions, interests, aspirations, common to all members of the society. This is necessary to the national consciousness: we may call it, if we like, in the words of Rousseau, national character. He maintains that, 'Chaque nation a son caractère propre et spécifique',[1] and his practical application of this idea might well be regarded as one of the most original aspects of his political thinking.

As at so many other points, Rousseau's forerunner here too is Montesquieu, who also recognizes the existence of 'l'esprit général d'une nation', a product, he says, of the influence of climate and religion, laws, government, the experiences of the past, manners and customs, which is in fact the national character. But Montesquieu draws no deductions of political importance; and although in a sense his whole argument leads up to the realization that this must be the essential basis of political life, he never recognizes it explicitly· The idea of the *esprit général* is overshadowed because of the great emphasis he lays on the single factor of climate; whereas with Rousseau the national character in the widest sense of the term becomes the

[1] *Œuvres*, v. 390: *Émile*, V.

foundation of political life and the real source of the strength of the state. 'La première règle, que nous avons à suivre,' he says when he has to set about drawing up a constitution for an actual state, 'c'est le caractère national: tout peuple a, ou doit avoir, un caractère national; s'il en manquait, il faudrait commencer par le lui donner'.[1] It was because of the value he attached to the national character that Rousseau attacked the introduction of French customs into Switzerland, or criticized Peter the Great for trying to make Germans and English when what he really needed was Russians.[2]

It is not difficult to see that there is a certain contradiction in these ideas. It seems to be taken for granted that a national character is a natural and unfailing attribute of every people; yet at the same time that it is something which it is necessary to create and with which it is the duty of the ruler to endow his people. One is forced to conclude that while Rousseau holds that a people ought to have a national character, its existence cannot necessarily be predicated of every society. It represents thus an ideal as well as a fact. The particular character which it is assumed that each people should have is dictated partly by what is appropriate to the actual circumstances of the state and partly by the ideal which the legislator sets before himself.

Whether an unconscious growth or a deliberate achievement, the first question we have necessarily to ask of Rousseau is in what way he accounts for the existence of national differences. We have to glean his positive ideas of what constitutes national character from various sources, but especially from his essays on the constitutions of Corsica and Poland. His discussion of the origins of nationality rejects what was destined to be the favourite nineteenth-century explanation, the division of mankind into races. The original races, if there were such, have been, he says, 'tellement transplanté et confondu' that a pure one hardly exists on the face of the earth, unless it be in the depth of Africa.[3] He is disposed to attribute a larger part to language: each language he believes has its particular spirit and characteristics, which may be in part allied to the differences of national character, though whether as cause or effect he is unable to

[1] Pol. Writings, ii. 319: Proj. Corse.
[2] id., ii. 56: Con. soc., II. viii; cf. Corr. Gén., ix. 9.
[3] id., i. 355: Fragments.

decide.[1] He begins by conceding the initial influence of natural surroundings on the primitive character of the inhabitants. Thus it is that he derives the national character of the Swiss from their mountainous home. In the well-known letter of Saint-Preux he is surely describing his own sentiments when he exclaims, 'Plus j'approchais de la Suisse, plus je me sentais ému. L'instant où, des hauteurs du Jura je découvris le lac de Genève fut un instant d'extase et de ravissement. La vue de mon pays, de ce pays si chéri où des torrents de plaisirs avaient inondé mon cœur; l'air des Alpes si salutaire et si pur; le doux air de la patrie, plus suave que les parfums de l'orient; cette terre riche et fertile, ce paysage unique, le plus beau dont l'œil humain fut jamais frappé; . . . tous cela me jettait dans des transports que je ne puis décrire, et semblait me rendre à la fois la jouissance de ma vie entière.'[2]

But it is only in the remote countryside that national character exists uncorrupted.[3] All great capitals are alike, he observes in the Emile; 'C'est la campagne qui fait le pays, et c'est le peuple de la campagne qui fait la nation'.[4] One can perhaps trace the influence of Montesquieu in an observation that when a country is not peopled by colonists it is from the nature of the soil that the primitive character of the inhabitants is born.[5] But, however originated, the association of national affections with the physical environment is clearly marked for Rousseau. 'Les paysans,' he believes, 'sont attachés à leur sol beaucoup plus que les citadins à leurs villes . . . De là le contentement de son état, qui rend l'homme paisible; de là l'amour de la patrie, qui l'attache à sa constitution.'[6] He holds that among the ancients national character was more strongly developed, when a people occupied its territory for so long that it forgot there ever was a time when its ancestors had been strangers come to settle on the soil.

In modern Europe, however, the close relationships between the various states, following on the migrations of the nations,

---

[1] Œuvres, v. 427: Émile, V.
[2] Nouv. Hél., iii. 156.
[3] id., ii. 324.
[4] Œuvres, v. 424: Émile, V.
[5] Pol. Writings, ii. 320: Proj. Corse.
[6] id., ii. 310-11: Proj. Corse.

have produced a confusion of races and peoples, a cosmopolitan medley, from which it resulted, he wrote, that a Frenchman, an Englishman, a Spaniard, an Italian, a Russian are all in effect the same man.[1] From this one may possibly trace the element in which his theory differed most widely from the ideas of the other great contemporary thinker to anticipate the coming of the age of nationality, Edmund Burke. For Montesquieu national character had been almost purely a result of physical environment; for Burke the national character shapes for itself the institutions of the country; whereas Rousseau, as we have seen, looking at the weakness of national consciousness in his age, takes the institutions as themselves instruments by which the national character can be moulded and indeed created, and a love of country inspired. Nationality is no longer, as with Montesquieu, merely a political *datum*, a result of the operation of natural forces that has to be accepted as beyond the power of human interference. Once again we discover the peculiar quality of Rousseau's thinking, which does not lie so much in the novelty of his analysis, as in the fact that he brings under the dominion of the human will forces that most previous and contemporary thinkers had treated as autonomous. He assumes that national character can be created. 'Ce sont les institutions nationales qui forment le génie, le caractère, les goûts et les mœurs d'un peuple . . . qui lui inspirent cet ardent amour de la patrie.'[2] Rousseau admitted of course the complex nature of the relation between national character and institutions; the institutions had to be adapted to the nation, while at the same time the nation was shaped by the institutions;[3] yet in so far as it was possible to attribute any priority it was to the institutions that he gave it. In the long run, he believed, peoples are what their governments make them.[4]

It would be doing Rousseau an injustice to give the impression that he attributed the formation of national character solely to the influence of physical surroundings and political institutions. It is a product of the environment as a whole, and in this connection the influence of education has particularly to be considered.

[1] *Pol. Writings*, ii. 438: *Gouv. Pol.*
[2] *id.*, ii. 431: *Gouv. Pol.*
[3] *id.*, ii. 307: *Proj. Corse.*
[4] *id.*, i. 248: *Écon. pol.*

There is not, it is true, a great distinction here, because for Rousseau the end of the state and the object of all its institutions is essentially and in the broadest sense the education of the citizens, and in his ideal state, a somewhat imaginary Sparta, the education of the children is the chief concern of the constitution.[1] When he is asked by what institutions the distinctive characteristics of the nations are developed, his answer is that it is education which elevates the individual to national status.[2] 'C'est par elle qu'on formera de bonne heure les jeunes citoyens à réunir toutes leurs passions dans l'amour de la patrie, toutes leurs volontés dans la volonté générale.'[3] For this reason the education of children, the fitting them for their future duties as citizens, cannot be left at the mercy of the prejudices of their parents. A system of public education, under rules and teachers provided by the state, is, he says, a fundamental maxim of all legitimate government.[4] It is as necessary, in addition, for the functioning of free institutions as for the development of a national character.

An apparent contradiction has frequently been pointed out between Rousseau's insistence on a public education for the citizen and his own treatise on education, in which Emile receives a strictly private education. The explanation is equally familiar, that in the corrupt society of the eighteenth century the requisites for a public education being lacking, the tutor takes the place of the state and performs those duties which it is incapable of fulfilling. Vaughan indicates another apparent discrepancy, the absence of any scheme for a national education from the *Contrat social*. One cannot explain this by the theory that Rousseau only realized the importance of national education at the end of his life, when his ideas on the nation state were developed most fully, as in the *Gouvernement de Pologne*, since it is to be found with almost equal emphasis in the *Economie politique*. One can only assume, with Vaughan, that it arises from the more limited scope of the *Contrat social*,[5] where he confines himself almost exclusively to the sphere of political

[1] *id.*, i. 190: *Disc. inég.*
[2] *id.*, ii. 437: *Gouv. Pol.*
[3] *id.*, i. 277: *Écon. pol.; cf. id.*, i. 319: *Fragments;* i. 255: *Écon. pol.*
[4] *id.*, i. 256-7: *Écon. pol.*
[5] *id.*, i. 232.

institutions; his object is the strictly limited one of discussing the form of political organization capable of securing freedom in the state.

The *Economie politique*, on the other hand, is a broader if slighter study. But perhaps the most satisfactory explanation of the absence of the idea of national education from the *Contrat social* is that while the *Corsica* and the *Poland* are directed to the immediate practical end of saving the state by strengthening the nation, the *Contrat social* takes for granted the existence of a keen desire on the part of the members of the state to belong to the same community, or as we would call it, national feeling; and it concerns itself only with the philosophical justification and the political organization of the state, the emotional basis of which is pre-supposed.

When Rousseau speaks of national education, the term has to be understood in the broadest sense. It is not the rather negative enlightenment of the *philosophes*, the object of which was primarily the removal of superstition and prejudices. It is an education of the character rather than of the intellect, but this is the only respect in which it coincides with the education of Emile. To attempt to reconcile finally the patriotic scheme of education with the more philosophical ideal propounded in the *Emile* is a hopeless effort. As Rousseau himself observes, it is necessary to choose between the man and the citizen. One cannot, he believes, educate at the same time for the two ideals.[1] Whereas Emile, the citizen of the world, has to be guarded from the prejudices and passions roused by the study of that most dangerous of all subjects, history, the young patriot is to be soaked in the history of his country. How great a development this represents from Rousseau's ideas even as late as the *Nouvelle Héloïse*, is demonstrated by the precepts of Saint-Preux, who it is true would allow Julie to study the history of her own country, but only because of its freedom and simplicity, because there she would find the history of modern men with classical virtues. But those who dare to maintain that the most interesting history and the most valuable study is always the history of one's own country the generous Saint-Preux strictly confutes.[2]

[1] *Pol. Writings*, ii. 144; *Emile*.
[2] *Nouv. Hél.*, ii. 49.

H

Because we have mentioned history, it must not be supposed that the patriotic education, as Rousseau conceived it, was to be a mere academic discipline confined to the orthodox methods of the schools. The humblest means were not to be despised. 'Par où donc émouvoir les cœurs, et faire aimer la patrie et ses lois? . . . Par des jeux d'enfants: par des institutions oiseuses aux yeux des hommes superficiels, mais qui forment des habitudes chéries et des attachements invincibles.'[1] Religion also has its part to play in the formation of national spirit, as, says Rousseau, is proved by the history of the Jews, who, dispersed and in exile, yet remained a nation through the power of cohesion their religion gave them. The sanctity of the nation must be impressed on its members even if it is necessary to call in the aid of what otherwise would be considered 'frivolous and superstitious rites'.[2] These are the instruments with which the state can create and utilize that great force of national public opinion, so skilfully put into operation by classical statesmen and totally ignored, he fears, by modern rulers.[3]

What, we may ask again, is the idea of the nation which results from all this? It is clearly something more than the patriotism of the *ancien régime,* indeed the idea of loyalty to a territorial system hardly enters into question. What makes the nation is the community of its members. It is the men, he had said in the *Contrat social,* who constitute the state.[4] This is what justifies the claim that in Rousseau is found the idea of the change from *roi de France* into *roi des Français,*[5] which appeared in the Constitution of 1791. But Rousseau goes beyond the individual members of the nation when he seeks its essential nature. 'Où est-elle cette patrie?' he asks, and replies, 'Ce ne sont ni les murs ni les hommes qui font la patrie: ce sont les loix, les mœurs, les coutumes, le Gouvernement, la constitution, la manière d'être qui resulte de tout cela. La patrie est dans les relations de l'Etat à ses membres; quand ces rélations changent ou s'anéantissent, la patrie s'évanouit.' 'Ainsi, Monsieur,' he concludes, for he is thinking of his own Geneva and the illegal

[1] Pol. Writings, ii. 427: Gouv. Pol.; cf. id., ii. 439.
[2] id., ii. 429: Gouv. Pol.
[3] id., i. 322: Fragments.
[4] id., ii. 58: Con. soc., II. x.
[5] Mercier, op. cit., ii. 308-9.

condemnation doled out to him by the reigning oligarchy, 'pleurons la nôtre; elle a péri.'[1]

In the times that were coming on the idea of the nation was to be far more than a contribution to political theory: in the development of nationalism facts ran away from theories. Nor indeed did Rousseau himself envisage nationality merely as a theoretical idea. It should be remembered that in the two works from which most of our knowledge of his ideas on this subject is drawn his aim is severely practical. He is not concerned with patriotism as an ideal: his aim is to indicate the means by which Corsica and Poland may defend themselves against their enemies and preserve their independence. 'La vertu de ses citoyens, leur zèle patriotique, la forme particulière que des institutions nationales peuvent donner à leurs âmes, voilà le seul rempart toujours prêt à la défendre, et qu'aucune armèe ne saurait forcer.'[2] His *amour de la patrie* is here but another name for what we should call nationalism. The trend of his ideas leads straight to the nineteenth-century theory of national self-determination, which in a manuscript note he puts quite explicitly. 'Qu'on puisse à son gré faire passer les peuples de maître en maître, comme des troupeaux de bétail, sans consulter ni leur intérêt ni leur avis, c'est se moquer des gens de le dire sérieusement.'[3] One cannot but be reminded again of Burke, and his comment on the transference of the island of Corsica from Genoa to France: 'Thus was a nation disposed of without its consent, like the trees on an estate'.[4]

---

[1] *Corr. Gén.*, x. 337-8, March 1, 1764. The same idea of the nation, though in a more elaborate form, is found equally in the other great prophet of the romantic movement in politics, Burke. It is therefore only to be expected that we should remark its influence in the theocratic school, which derived—at least in part—from both Rousseau and Burke. In de Maistre it assumes a somewhat rigid form, 'Il faut que les dogmes religieux et politiques mêlés et confondus forment ensemble une *raison universelle* ou *nationale* assez forte pour réprimer les aberrations de la raison individuelle. . . . Qu'est ce que le *patriotisme?* c'est cette raison nationale dont je parle' (de Maistre, *Œuvres*, 1884-6, i. 375-7: *Étude sur la souveraineté*). Bonald uses language he might have borrowed from Burke. 'L'homme civilisé ne voit la patrie que dans les lois qui régissent la société, dans l'ordre qui y règne, dans les pouvoirs qui la gouvernent, dans la religion qu'on y professe, et pour lui son pays peut n'être pas toujours sa patrie.' (Bonald, *Œuvres*, 1852, ii. 664: *De l'Émigration*.)

[2] *Pol. Writings*, ii. 431: *Gouv. Pol.*

[3] *id.*, i. 340-1.

[4] *Annual Register*, 1768, Historical Section, p. 2.

To say that Rousseau was a prophet of the national movement is not necessarily to claim that he exercised any influence over its practical development: the causes of that are to be found in the sphere of actual events and in the spirit of a new age. But Rousseau, like Burke, was more conscious than others of the stirrings in the air, of the springtime of a new world. He not only wrote the words that spelt the doom of the *ancien régime*, but also prophesied the national state of the future which was to take its place.

3. NATIONALISM, THE NEW TYRANNY

Rousseau is to be regarded, as we have seen, as the upholder of political freedom against the despotic monarchies of the eighteenth century. Even in the *Contrat social* his object is to provide a theoretical basis for political liberty, and it is at least arguable that he is not so unsuccessful as has sometimes been alleged. But does he appear in the same light in relation to the new nation state, which embodied his practical ideal in politics, or does he in the last resort merely change one despotism for another, setting up in the name of the nation a tyranny more terrible and all-embracing than that of kings? Against the oecumenical, humanitarian ideas which form the noblest element in Voltaire's political creed he puts forward an ideal of patriotism which appears hard and exclusive to the utmost degree. As he writes, coldly and unemotionally, 'L'esprit patriotique est un esprit exclusif qui nous fait regarder comme étranger et presque comme ennemi tout autre que nos con-citoyens'.[1] This he admits to be a defect, but an inevitable one and not of the greatest importance. The essential thing, he says, is to be good to the people with whom one lives.[2] Clearly the nationalist wars which were to re-draw the frontiers of Europe with blood, and to write the history of an ideal in war and devastation, do not enter into the scope of his thought. In proclaiming the blind and arrogant hostility of the patriot to all that is alien, Rousseau, it might be said, is merely stating a fact; but this will not serve as an excuse, because he is no less extreme in expressing his view of what ought to be. 'Un enfant, en

[1] *Pol. Writings*, ii. 166: to Usteri, April 30, 1763; cf. *id.*, ii. 144.
[2] *id.*, ii. 144-5: *Émile*

ouvrant les yeux, doit voir la patrie, et jusqu'à la mort ne doit plus voir qu'elle.'[1]

This eulogy of national exclusiveness forms a striking contradiction to Rousseau's often repeated denunciation of war. Otherwise, as a prophet of international peace he would deserve possibly even more credit than Voltaire, despite the satire of *Candide*, and this not merely because of Rousseau's attempt to revive Saint-Pierre's project for international peace, but because of the views he consistently maintained on the problem of international relations and war. These may be summarized very briefly. In the first place, Rousseau proclaimed the existing evil condition of international relations, in fact the reign of anarchy in Europe—wars which nobody wanted and which desolated the whole world, immense armies kept up in peace time yet incapable of safeguarding the country in war, ministers who were overwhelmed with labours yet achieved nothing, mysterious, futile treaties, alliances painfully built up by years of negotiation, and broken off in a single day: such is his summary.[2] As for the pretended *droit des gens* which is supposed to moderate the violence of war and the unscrupulousness of diplomacy, its laws, says Rousseau, are the merest chimeras, more remote from reality than the law of nature itself.[3] The result of continual warfare and unrest is the development of the system of large standing armies, which exhaust the revenues of the state and provide a perpetual temptation to the government to utilize them in aggressive war.[4]

This is Rousseau's description of the actual state of international relations. But the warlike condition is, according to him, not natural to the human species. Man seems to him naturally peaceable and timid. 'Ce n'est qu'après avoir fait société avec quelque homme qu'il se détermine à en attaquer un autre; et il ne devient soldat qu'après avoir été citoyen.'[5] There is no war between men, but only between states. Already in the *Discours sur l'inégalité* he had traced the origin of war and its attendant horrors to the effect of the division of the human race into

[1] *Pol. Writings*, ii. 437: *Gouv. Pol.*
[2] id., i. 314: *Fragments; cf. id.*, i. 182, 204: *Disc. inég.*
[3] id., i. 304: *L'état de guerre.*
[4] id., i. 383; *Paix perpét.; cf. id.*, i. 265: *Écon. pol.*; ii. 486: *Gouv. Pol.*
[5] id., i. 294: *L'état de guerre.*

different societies.[1] Why then, the query inevitably arises, in the face of all the evil resulting from the conflicts of states, does he glorify the division of the world into nations, encourage them to develop the particularist spirit in its highest degree, and thus intensify existing evils? We might argue that Rousseau is compelled to accept the existence of separate national states by the impossibility of the formation of a universal society, which he admits.[2] But his nationalism is no passive acceptance of facts, it is a positive glorification of them. Have we to conclude, then, that we can clear Rousseau from the accusation of being the inspirer of the Terrorists, only to make him the prophet of the insane nationalism of the twentieth century?

There is a still more serious criticism to be brought against this aspect of his political theory, in respect of its reactions on the liberty of the individual. A significant connection may be remarked here between the two most illiberal of Rousseau's political principles, the idea of nationality and that of the civil religion. The real case for regarding him as an enemy of liberal Europe comes back almost inevitably to these ideas, which are closely associated, because the civil religion is the religion of the state, of such a state as is upheld by Rousseau's nationalism, for the sake of which in fact it exists. Moreover nationalism as expounded in the *Poland* comes sometimes perilously near to being the rule of prejudice and of mass emotion.

It is difficult in our day not to envisage nationalism in terms of those movements which in its name have established the government of organized violence and mass hysteria. The defect which vitiates the application of this form of criticism to Rousseau, however, is that it involves judging a political force by the uses to which it was destined to be put a century and a half later. Possibilities for both evil and good were present in the nationalist movement from the very beginning. The apology for Rousseau must be based on the conditions of his day, when the great international menace seemed to be the aggressive imperialism of the large powers, the apparently insatiable lust for increased territory exhibited by the rulers of Prussia and Russia and France in Europe and by England overseas. This evil

[1] *id.*, i. 182.

[2] *id.*, i. 449-50: *Con. soc.* (first version). It is worth noting, however, that this passage was cancelled.

Rousseau attributed not to any aggressive nationalist sentiment in the peoples of these countries but primarily to their defective forms of government. A despotic ruler can always secure the support of the people for a forward foreign policy if he has the least ability or good luck, and he is likely to wish to do so, because the appeal to nationalist passions appears to be the surest means by which in modern times a people can be kept for a prolonged period in a state of blind obedience. If it was useful to the old-fashioned despot, who could at least fall back on the support of traditional loyalty, it was to become almost indispensable to the modern dictator. But it is only fair to remark that, as Rousseau would have us note, in these cases the menace to peace springs less from the nationalism of the people than from the political necessities of the ruler.

As for the militarism and international anarchy of the eighteenth century, these are evils, Rousseau would say, resulting directly from the absence of genuine nations and national feeling. 'L'Etat, . . . étant un corps artificiel, n'a nulle mesure déterminé. . . . Sa sûreté, sa conservation, demandent qu'il se rend plus puissant que tous ses voisins.' [1] A heterogeneous collection of 'subjects', it could have no natural limits, such as a consistent theory of nationality imposed, and its preservation—as the will of the people was not to be relied upon—depended entirely on its military strength. It was as an alternative to this method of holding the state together that Rousseau appealed to national feeling. Its function was essentially a non-aggressive one. Of Poland, as earlier of Corsica, he wrote that, 'Une seule chose suffit pour la rendre impossible à subjuguer: l'amour de la patrie et de la liberté'. [2] Militarism ceases to rule under such conditions, because in a state where these sentiments prevail mercenary armies are not needed: a national militia composed of the citizens themselves will defend their frontiers. [3] Basing himself on the experience of Rome and the ancient city states and of Switzerland in modern times, Rousseau urges strongly the case for a citizen army as against a professional one. 'Tous les Citoyens doivent être soldats par devoir, aucun par métier.' [4]

---

[1] Pol. Writings, i. 297: L'état de guerre.
[2] id., ii. 491: Gouv. Pol.; cf. id., ii. 431.
[3] id., 486-8: Gouv. Pol.
[4] Nouv. Hél., ii. 310, n.

Practically all the *philosophes* were in agreement with him here, notably Montesquieu and Mably; and yet once again we have to remark that what seemed a patent truth at one moment was to lose its validity in the course of a generation. The citizen army which seemed to be a guarantee of liberty became in the hands of Napoleon the greatest instrument of military despotism.

Rousseau advocated this citizen army mainly from internal reasons. But even if the wars of republics were bitterer than those of monarchies, he took it for granted that the nations would not indulge in the irresponsible wars of the despots. According to a report by Mercier he said in 1775, 'Les nations ne se battent que pour un grand et véritable intérêt; tandis que les princes agissent par orgueil'.[1] It follows from Rousseau's conception of the state as a definite entity with a general will and a distinct national spirit that it has certain assigned limits which it cannot exceed. Imperial ambitions are bound to be fatal to the liberty of the nation, he writes of England, and here he employs precisely the argument against despotic rule that I have just outlined. 'Le goût des conquêtes . . . n'a pas tant pour véritable motif le désir apparent d'agrandir la nation que le désir caché d'augmenter au dedans l'autorité des chefs, à l'aide de l'augmentation des troupes et à la faveur de la diversion que font les objets de la guerre dans l'esprit des citoyens.'[2] What concerned the citizen, he believed, was to be governed justly and peaceably: in the glory and power of the state he had no interest.[3]

Obviously the dangers of aggressive nationalism are not anticipated by Rousseau. That the reshaping of Europe into national states might cause more bloodshed than the wars of the despots, that citizen armies might be more formidable and far larger than mercenary ones, that national wars might be more terrible than those resulting from the ambitions of kings, was a secret hidden from him. In his anxiety to promote the national spirit of the Poles he lays himself fairly open to the criticism of Bonald. 'Cet ami de l'humanité insiste beaucoup trop, pour l'honneur de la philosophie, ainsi que Mably, sur la nécessité d'exciter, d'éterniser dans le coeur des Polonais la haine contre leur voisins.'[4]

---

[1] Mercier, *op. cit.*, ii. 210-11.
[2] *Pol. Writings*, i. 263-4: *Écon. pol.*
[3] *id.*, i. 398, n. 1: *Polysynodie*.
[4] Bonald, *Œuvres*, 1859, ii. 436.

In order to be just to Rousseau, however, we must take the national idea not in all its subsequent developments and aberrations, but as he envisaged it. In itself it is an emotion which we can hardly either approve or condemn without knowing its particular application. As G. M. Trevelyan said, 'The sentiment of nationality, that simplest of all ideals which appeals to the largest quantity of brute force, has in its nature no political affinities either with liberty on the one hand or with tyranny on the other; it can be turned by some chance current of events, or by the cunning or clumsiness of statesmen, to run in any channel and to work any wheel'.[1] The evils of modern nationalism are at least not the necessary result of the national idea as Rousseau conceived it. We may go farther and claim indeed that he provided in advance the corrective to some of its most dangerous features.

The sentiment of nationality, he believes, comes in the beginning from attachment to the land on which one lives. For this very reason it is likely to be a conservative, defensive force rather than an aggressive one. In the second place, he believed, not altogether correctly, that the sentiment of nationality is necessarily strongest in small states, and weakest in large ones with widely separated and diversified territories. His preference for the small state has already been discussed. He can hardly be accused of ignoring the evil consequences that would flow from the wars of the great nation states when he has written, 'Grandeur des nations, étendue des Etats: première et principale source des malheurs du genre humain'.[2] Rousseau's patriotism has been called le patriotisme de clocher. This kind of nationalism is perhaps narrow, exclusive, provincial; but it has little in common with the national imperialisms, the racial megalomania, of later times. The danger which Rousseau's form of nationalism presents is quite the reverse. The small states which alone he admires, though stronger in proportion to their size than great ones, are necessarily at the mercy of their larger neighbours. If his examination of the constitution of the various states of Europe leads him to the conclusion that some are too large to be well governed, it also reveals to him that others are too small to be able to maintain their independence.[3]

[1] G. M. Trevelyan, England under the Stuarts, 1904, p. 117.
[2] Pol. Writings, ii. 442: Gouv. Pol.   [3] id., i. 321: Fragments.

As Windenberger has shown, he has a remedy for this defect, and one which serves to emphasize the essentially non-aggressive nature of his nationalism.[1] It is to be found in the federal system, 'Le seul qui réunisse les avantages des grands et des petits États'.[2] The question Rousseau puts himself here is practically identical in form with that which provided the starting-point for the *Contrat social*, to find 'une forme de Gouvernement confédérative, qui, unissant les peuples par des liens semblables à ceux qui unissent les individus, soumette également les uns et les autres à l'autorité des lois'.[3] This scheme has been criticized from the legal standpoint, on the ground that the idea of federation is irreconcilable with the idea of the personality of the state, and with the principle of national sovereignty; but this only serves to show once more the contrast between Rousseau's idea of the state and the legal theory of sovereignty. For Rousseau the submission of the state to the rule of law by the introduction of a system of federation no more limits its real liberty than the social contract limits the liberty of individuals: all it does is to substitute the reign of law freely accepted for an involuntary anarchy. Far from destroying national independence it is intended to be its safeguard. The necessary conclusion is that Rousseau's system of national sovereignty is less absolute than his critics have supposed.

Once again, we see that the possibility of an aggressive national spirit is not conceived by Rousseau. The idea of conquest or domination is in fact in contradiction with his whole attitude. He accepts nationality as a political fact and as a force capable of maintaining the independence of the state. In the eighteenth century, at the height of the age of partitions, and in a work devoted to Poland, it was natural that the latter should be the leading consideration. But it is clear that fundamentally for Rousseau nationality is a spiritual force which he regards as necessary for the mental well-being of individuals in the state and essential to their self-respect. The basic fact is not political allegiance to a government, it is membership of a community, the sharing of a common way of life, a manner of being, as he puts it. Admittedly we do not find this point of

---

[1] J. L. Windenberger, *La république confédérative des petits États*, 1900.
[2] *Pol. Writings*, ii. 443: *Gouv. Pol.*
[3] *id.*, i. 365: *Paix perpét.*; cf. *id.*, ii. 158: *Émile*.

view developed at length in his works. It was only definitely
evoked towards the end of his life and by the special circumstances surrounding the Polish question, though the seeds are
to be found much earlier.

A letter[1] from the manuscripts of his self-styled friend and
disciple, the comte d'Antraigues, carries forward the argument
for us. Whether the letter be based on one from the pen of
Rousseau, or whether it be wholly a fabrication of d'Antraigues
remains in doubt, though if it be attributed to d'Antraigues he
certainly deserves a somewhat higher rank as a political thinker
than he has usually been given.[2] But if not by Rousseau himself,
the letter was at least composed under the influence of his ideas,
and by one who is to be reckoned a fervent and whole-hearted
disciple. It is not without significance that the letter should
derive the conception of nationality, or, as it is termed here,
l'amour du pays natal, from reflections on the Middle Ages, the
time when, the writer says, sensibility and religion reigned
over the human heart, and when the highest ideals of chivalry
were the fortunate effect arising from what the enlightened
eighteenth century would have called illusions. The connection
thus established provides us with a valuable indication of the
way in which the idea of nationality developed. It is perfectly
true that the medieval revival precedes, though by very little,
the birth of the national idea, and that both form part of the
general romantic movement. In England those thinkers who are
notable for their early apprehension of the national idea—
Burke, with Wordsworth and the other Lake Poets—share also
in the new-born admiration for the Middle Ages. One derives
from the d'Antraigues letter a hint that the association perhaps
goes deeper, that the medieval revival is not merely one mani-
festation of the new phase of thought, but also partly the cause
of the new attitude towards politics.

From where but from the Middle Ages might those who
believed in nationality have drawn their ultimate inspiration?
Classical history abounds with examples of patriotism, and
Rousseau made ample use of them, but—whether he realized
it himself or not—his idea of a national spirit is fundamentally
different from the patriotism of the ancient world. Europe from

[1] See Appendix II.
[2] See Appendix I.

the sixteenth century onwards was too completely under the influence of classical thought and of the struggle for territorial aggrandizement to provide scope for the development of the idea of nationality. The Middle Ages on the other hand were the time of the making of the nations. The chaos of the latter centuries of the Roman Empire witnessed their birth throes, and by the end of the medieval period the national divisions of Europe were fairly completely sketched out as we have them now. In practice most of the nations which have won or regained their independence during the last century have looked back to their medieval greatness for inspiration. It was natural that the theorists of the national movement should have been the first to hark back to the time when the nations were being created, and perhaps at any rate in part to discover the idea itself hidden in the records of medieval history.

But the point at which the letter most strikingly carries on and develops Rousseau's own ideas is in the distinction it draws between *l'amour de la patrie* and *l'amour du pays natal*, a distinction which well illustrates the difference between the classical eighteenth-century idea of patriotism and the modern idea of nationality. How far removed at an earlier date Rousseau was from any preference for the latter is shown in the *Nouvelle Héloïse*, when Claire, after exclaiming how beautiful it was to have a *patrie*, added, 'et Dieu garde de mal tous ceux qui pensent en avoir une, et n'ont pourtant qu'un pays!'[1] A passage from the *Emile*, however, indicates other ideas on this subject. 'Qui n'a pas une patrie, a du moins un pays. . . . Ne dis donc pas, que m'importe où que je sois? Il t'importe d'être où tu peux remplir tous tes devoirs, et l'un de ces devoirs est l'attachement pour le lieu de ta naissance. Tes compatriotes te protégèrent enfant, tu dois les aimer étant homme.'[2] We seem to detect here the beginning of a conscious distinction between the classical ideal of patriotism and the newer ideal of nationality, a distinction which becomes quite explicit in the d'Antraigues letter. The former is the exclusive patriotism which makes the citizen regard with enmity all who are not of his own nation, and to this the author of the letter very definitely prefers what he calls *l'amour du pays natal*, that sentiment which, springing from

[1] *Nouv. Hél.*, iv. 205.
[2] *Œuvres*, v. 433-4; *Emile*, V.

our earliest associations, from the soil on which we live, from the affection with which we are surrounded in childhood, from the ideals of youth, and the aspirations of manhood, is a natural growth and knows nothing of the artificial hatreds and wars of governments and states. Whether Rousseau himself ends here, or whether we are indebted to d'Antraigues for drawing the conclusion, it is only just to observe before we leave this subject that his national principles could lead as naturally in this direction as they could in the direction of that fanatical nationalism which by adopting the worst vices of imperialism seems to provide itself its own condemnation.

CHAPTER V

THE SOCIAL IDEAL

1. LUXE: ROUSSEAU AGAINST VOLTAIRE

If we confine our attention exclusively to political matters we necessarily fail to understand Rousseau's ideas to the fullest degree. He is in truth as much a social as a political reformer. Fundamentally, despite the impression one is apt to disengage from the *Contrat social*, the individual interested him more than the state. His national ideals may seem to sacrifice the individual to the nation, but even here without the individual the nation is nothing, it exists for the spiritual well-being of its members. To reach the heart of Rousseau's conception of society, then, we must come down to the life of the individual, and this, as he is one of the first to recognize, is determined as much by economic as by political considerations. Rousseau was not, of course, an economist. but that did not prevent him from having definite ideas on the economic structure of society. These ideas are, however, based primarily on considerations of a moral order; in fact he completely passes by the strictly economic point of view. Just as in the political field his object is neither power nor sovereignty, so here what he is concerned with is not the maximization of wealth, whether of individuals or of the community, but the achievement of the good life. To determine what constitutes in practice the good life it is necessary to have a scale of social values, and in working this out Rousseau begins, as he does in the political order, with an initial judgment on the society he had in front of him.

Whether it be attributed to his modest origins, to his early training in vagabondage, his experience as a lacquey in Italy, the comparative ill success of his first attempts to enter the Parisian literary world, his alleged *gaucherie* in the salons of the great, or to a native ingredient in his character, not to be traced to any particular set of circumstances but belonging to the nature of the man himself, whatever be the cause, he exhibits consistently an attitude of distrust and suspicion towards the rich and the powerful. It can be found in an early poem of 1742,

> Quoi! de vils parchemins, par faveur obtenus,
> Leur donneront le droit de vivre sans vertus![1]

A year before this he had written himself down a proud republican, who repulsed the arrogant patronage of the rich.[2] In a somewhat later poem he exclaimed,

> Point de Crésus, point de canaille;
> Point surtout de cette racaille,
> Que l'on appelle grands Seigneurs,
> Fripons sans probité, sans mœurs,
>
> .   .   .   .   .   .
>
> Mangeant fièrement notre bien;
> Exigeant tout, n'accordant rien.[3]

Such outbursts are more significant than the attack on inequality in the Second Discourse, which might otherwise be explained away as a literary exercise, as indeed contemporary opinion seems to have regarded it. The absence of any attempt to suppress a work so extreme in its criticism of social institutions and so violent in its language can only be accounted for on the assumption that for a long time few of its readers realized that it was meant to be taken in earnest. Even today apologists have tried to discount the significance of his diatribe against inequality, to write it down as a simple *boutade*. But it is borne out by everything he wrote on the subject, and finally by his life itself. 'Tous les avantages de la société,' he complains bitterly, 'ne sont-ils pas pour les puissants et les riches?'[4] In this field we cannot fail to describe Rousseau as a revolutionary. Here at least he was the Jean-Jacques of legend, whose whole life was a protest against a system of society which he regarded as thoroughly rotten, a declaration of war against the established order.

To treat Rousseau's campaign merely as an attack on a certain literary clique or a particular social caste, is to do him an injustice; nor is it even enough to say that he was attacking a system of social relationships. Essentially, it was not the system that tolerated a privileged *noblesse*, but the whole attitude to life of

[1] *Œuvres*, xiii. 420: *Épitre à M. Parisot*, 1742.
[2] *id.*, xiii. 413: *Épitre à M. Bordes*, 1741.
[3] *id.*, viii. 204: *Épitre à M. de l'Etang*, 1751.
[4] *Pol. Writings*, i. 267: *Écon. pol.*

his contemporaries which revolted him. His quarrel with society in fact was that it had one standard of values and he had another.

The eighteenth century was undoubtedly an age of 'materialism', and Rousseau, as is usual with those who are in revolt against the corruptions of society, appealed to the ideal of natural simplicity; but it will not do to jump to the conclusion that his protest was ascetic in inspiration, or based on any rooted hostility to material comfort. It was based partly on a sense of the injustice and the inequality with which material benefits were distributed, partly on a feeling of indignation at the corruption, the worthlessness of the society so unfairly endowed, but most of all on a profound conviction of the undesirability and even the wickedness of what the eighteenth century called *luxe*. On this point Rousseau came into conflict not only with the actual practice of the times, but with the economic theory of the physiocrats, and with the greatest of his enemies, the conscious advocate of luxury, Voltaire, whose poem, the *Mondain*, is the most famous of all its panegyrics.

> J'aime le luxe et même la mollesse,
> Tous les plaisirs, les arts de toute espèce;
> La propreté, le goût, les ornements.
> Toute honnête homme a de tels sentiments.

We must accept this as summing up Voltaire's attitude, even if the poem as a whole cannot be held to represent fairly his more mature moral theory. Moreover there is nothing out of the way in these views. Even Montesquieu, although occasionally seeming to praise simplicity of manners, as in the legendary history of the Troglodytes,[1] elsewhere appears much more strongly as a defender of the luxuries of civilization.

Despite, or possibly because of the criticism of Voltaire and the *philosophes*, Rousseau maintains his position consistently, and sometimes with apparently undue severity. From one of his outbursts, however, we can gain an insight into the reasons for which he took up such a definite stand. 'On croit m'embarrasser beaucoup,' he writes, 'en me demandant à quel point il faut borner le luxe. Mon sentiment est qu'il n'en faut point du tout. Tout est source de mal au delà du nécessaire physique. . . . Il

[1] *Lettres Persanes; cf. Esprit des Lois,* bk. VII. ch. II.

y a cent à parier contre un, que le premier qui porta des sabots était un homme punissable, à moins qu'il n'eût mal aux pieds.'[1] In spite of the conscious exaggeration of his illustration it is clear that the distinction Rousseau is drawing is between what is necessary for physical well-being and the luxuries which complicate life without, in his opinion, making it any better. Ultimately it is not the actual luxury in itself to which he objects so much as the attitude of mind it implies. Therefore he can agree that it is not to be extirpated by sumptuary legislation. 'C'est du fond des cœurs qu'il faut l'arracher,' he concludes, 'en y imprimant des goûts plus sains et plus nobles. . . . Les lois somptuaires irritent le désir par la contraite plutôt qu'elles ne l'éteignent par le châtiment.'[2] In the end Rouseau must be classed as fundamentally a moral reformer, and when he denounces *luxe* Calvinist Geneva can rightly claim him as one of her sons.

The attack on *luxe* is obviously connected with the idea of the return to nature. Economically 'back to nature' means back to the pastoral and agricultural existence. 'La condition naturelle à l'homme est de cultiver la terre et de vivre de ses fruits.'[3] After agriculture Rousseau would rank the necessary village crafts such as those of the blacksmith and the carpenter.[4] He is particularly an enemy to the life of the cities. Men were not made, he believes, to be heaped up like ants in great cities, where the physique is enfeebled and the manners corrupted, and where the race would perish if it were not constantly renewed from the country.[5] Hence, as his tutor instructs Emile, one of the ways in which a good man can offer an example to his fellows is by himself following the simple, rural life, the most natural and the happiest for those who have not been demoralized by the society of the towns.[6] It is not on account of any economic virtues that Rousseau upholds this ideal. He puts it forward on the ground of morality. Even more, we may be allowed to suspect, did the sentimental memories associated with the life he had led in the countryside endear it to him. 'Elle me transporte

[1] *Œuvres*, vii. 150: *Dernière réponse à M. Bordes.*
[2] *Pol. Writings*, ii. 437: *Gouv. Pol.*
[3] *Nouv. Hél.*, iv. 18.
[4] *Œuvres*, iv. 329-30: *Émile*, III.
[5] *id.*, iv. 48: *Émile*, I.
[6] *id.*, v. 435: *Émile*, V.

I

dans des habitations paisibles, au milieu de gens simples et bons, tels que ceux avec qui j'ai vécu jadis. Elle me rappelle et mon jeune âge, et mes innocents plaisirs.'[1]

The attack on *luxe* is hardly an economic idea, then; but if we turn to consider the positive economic principles of Rousseau, one finds that they are if anything more uncompromising than those of Calvin himself. He condemns finance and commerce wholeheartedly, regards the rentier as little better than a brigand, would abolish money, return to a system of barter, endow the state with a large public domain to avoid the necessity for taxes, and in so far as anything more might be needed for the public service take it in the form of *corvées*. He is thus not undeserving of the title of reactionary utopist, even if in stigmatizing the menace to the democratic state represented by the powers of finance he was not wholly mistaken. When he put forward his extremest ideas, he was legislating for Corsica, a small, primitive and isolated community. The *Poland* is in this and in many other respects much more moderate. We must remember also that Rousseau draws his economic ideas partly from the comparatively undeveloped Swiss communities, and partly from the ancient city state, particularly Sparta, the example of which, he says, he will never tire of quoting;[2] and he is applying them to the even more primitive society of Corsica. In the extreme form in which they were expressed in his proposals for a constitution for Corsica they exercised little or no influence, and although Rousseau doubtless intended them quite seriously we cannot regard them as of permanent value. Their exaggeration and impracticability merely detracted from the real moral force of his crusade.

2. THE IDEAL OF EQUALITY

It is far otherwise with Rousseau's attitude towards the idea of property, which is of necessity closely connected with those fundamental questions of the political organization of society which concern him so much. To begin with, we have to reckon with the sweeping attack on property in the Second Discourse. It is not so difficult to fit this in with Rousseau's later views on

---

[1] *Confessions, etc.*, iii. 247: *Promeneur solitaire*, VII.
[2] *Œuvres*, vi. 595: *Lett. à d'Alembert.*

the same subject as is sometimes supposed. Property is criticized by him as the source of inequality and of civil society, but just as he nowhere suggests abolishing society in order to return to a state of primitive virtue, so he does not propose to do away with property. He begins by thinking such a reversion impossible, and goes on to prove it undesirable. Civil society he has come to consider good because it is the source of men's moral feelings, and the property system may have equally fortunate results. Even in the Second Discourse what had aroused his antagonism were not social institutions in themselves, but the inequality resulting from them. Hence, as he directs his political thought to the preservation of political equality before the law, so in his economic writings he upholds economic equality.

He presupposes that the regulation of property, as of all other social institutions, is in the discretion of the legislative power. The sovereign has no right to touch the possessions of a particular individual or of one section of the community, but it has every right, according to Rousseau, to deal in any manner it pleases with the property system as a whole. When to this we add the rule laid down in the Project for Corsica, that the property of the state should be as extensive as possible and that of individuals on the contrary strictly limited,[1] and then recall the declarations in the *Economie politique* of the sacredness of property, we can understand why Vaughan declares that between the latter work and the essay on Corsica Rousseau has evolved from Lockian individualism to something hardly to be distinguished from socialism.[2]

And yet it is not so difficult to reconcile the two statements of his principles: for he never abandons the doctrine that property is or should be sacred. Is it not one of the first lessons that the careful tutor teaches the young Emile?[3] The happy effects of proprietorship are shown in the *Nouvelle Héloïse* by a comparison of the prosperity of the Vaud with the misery of Chablais. 'C'est ainsi, lui disais-je que la terre ouvre son sein fertile et prodigue ses trésors aux heureux peuples qui la cultivent pour eux-mêmes.' On the other hand the poverty, the half-cultivated fields on the opposite slopes bear witness that slaves

---

[1] *Pol. Writings*, ii. 337: *Proj. Corse.*

[2] *Du Contrat social*, ed. Vaughan, 1918, p. 133.

[3] *Œuvres*, iv. 126-9: *Émile*, II.

there till the land for an absentee master.[1] This is the argument
from experience. It is just what Arthur Young wrote, 'Give a
man the secure possession of a bleak rock, and he will turn it
into a garden; give him a nine years lease of a garden, and he
will convert it into a desert'.[2] The theoretical justification that
Rousseau offers for private property is practically identical with
that of Locke: the right of property is created when labour is
mixed with the products of nature, which in their natural condition are the common property of all mankind. 'L'idée de la
propriété remonte naturellement au droit de premier occupant
par le travail.'[3]

Locke apparently never realized the difficulty of getting from
what was to be later the somewhat dangerous labour theory of
value to the highly complicated, artificial property system of
Western Europe. Rousseau equally fails to remark the difficulty,
but for the simple reason that he does not attempt to effect the
transition. It is sometimes assumed that the Second Discourse
represents an extreme view on social questions which Rousseau
disavowed later. But he is no less emphatic in the *Emile*. 'Celui
qui mange dans l'oisiveté ce qu'il n'a pas gagné lui-même, le
vole; et un rentier que l'Etat paye pour ne rien faire ne diffère
guère, à mes yeux, d'un brigand qui vit aux dépens des passants.
. . . Travailler est donc un devoir indispensable à l'homme
social. Riche ou pauvre, puissant ou faible, tout citoyen oisif est
un fripon.'[4] With this to guide us it should be clear that when
Rousseau speaks of the sacredness of property he has in mind
only such property as he considers morally justified. It is the
property of the individual worker, of the peasant proprietor or
the craftsman, that he is anxious to safeguard.

Moreover his theory of property differs from Locke's in that
it is modified by the ideal of equality. Now property has a tendency to accumulate and become unequal, especially if one
admits an unrestricted right of inheritance. It is in this connection that Rousseau sees the necessity for the intervention of the
state. 'C'est précisément parce que la force des choses tend
toujours à détruire l'égalité, que la force de la législation doit

[1] *Nouv. Hél.*, iii. 280.
[2] Arthur Young, *Travels in France*, July 30, 1787.
[3] *Œuvres*, iv. 130: *Émile*, II.
[4] *id.*, iv. 329: *Émile*, III.

toujours tendre à la maintenir,'[1] Incidentally we may note that he does not base his argument on any visionary idea of human goodness, or suppose that a condition of approximate equality, even assuming it established, could be maintained without constant effort. In predicating the principle of equality he has in mind his ideal state, but what he says on this subject in the *Emile* does not lead one to suppose that he has much hope of seeing it put into practice. He confesses there that the universal tendency of the laws of all countries is to favour the strong against the weak, that the many are always sacrificed to the few and the interests of the community to those of individuals.[2]

Rousseau's economic equalitarianism, then, is not that sentimental faith in the natural equality of all men which represents an inability or unwillingness to face unpleasant facts. Even the desire for social justice does not provide his initial motive. Primarily he supports the principle of economic equality because he considers it necessary for the proper political functioning of his ideal state. He was a revolutionary in so far as he wished for the abolition of aristocratic privilege and the power of wealth; but looked at from the broader historical standpoint this did not imply the social revolution as it has been understood later, but rather the continuance and completion of that political revolution which began when feudal power was first repulsed from Swiss mountain retreats and Flemish city walls. Politically, Rousseau believes in the small owners of property, the middle classes, because he believes that it is only on them that the rule of law can be imposed with any hope of success. The laws, he says, are equally powerless against the treasures of the rich and the misery of the poor. Up to a point he allows that a moderate inequality is not necessarily harmful. In a monarchy it may be completely indifferent, but in a republic wealth will put its possessors above the laws and hence ruin the state.[3] It is worth noting that he arrives thus at a conclusion which is also very strongly upheld by Greek political philosophy. When, combined with this ideal, is the conviction, which plays so important a part in the upbringing of Emile, of the moral value of

[1] *Pol. Writings*, ii. 61: *Con. soc.*, II. xi.
[2] *Œuvres*, iv. 409 n.: *Émile*, IV.
[3] *Pol. Writings*, i. 254: *Écon. pol.*; cf *Œuvres*, vi. 571: *Lett. à d'Alembert*.

work, above all of manual labour, the resulting social theory can certainly not be a mere justification of things as they are.

Given the force of these views, it may astonish us that the *Discours sur l'inégalité* met with so little opposition, except from the *jejune* critics of 'back to nature', who took Rousseau quite literally and demanded why he did not retire to the woods or crawl about on all fours. But in fact these ideas on property were not exclusive to Rousseau, although perhaps expressed by him with greater force and literary power than by any other contemporary writer. Montesquieu, who, although attacked for his religious ideas, was certainly not regarded as socially subversive, has practically the same theory of property as Rousseau. In the works of many other writers, for instance, Raynal, Mercier, Mably and Helvétius, are to be found similar ideas, sometimes even in a more extreme form. 'At bottom,' to adopt the conclusion of Espinas, 'a single social conception possesses these writers, in appearance so diverse. It is, in the language of d'Argenson, that of a "ménagerie d'hommes heureux", of a little equalitarian republic, where the state regulates wealth at its pleasure, distributes land and dictates services to be demanded, presides over exchange, and takes care that there are on its territory neither rich nor poor nor idle.'[1]

Only on one point can I suggest a difference between Rousseau and these writers, in so far as he meant what he said, whereas for most of the others one cannot but suspect that equalitarian theories were little better than an academic exercise. Lichtenberger, in his conscientious study of socialism in the eighteenth century, concludes, indeed, that Meslier was the only genuine social revolutionary amongst them. If I would not insist on that title for Rousseau, at least I would claim that his ideas on this subject were something more than a reminiscence of the classics, that they were meant to have a practical effect, as indeed they did. Faguet takes Fourier, whom he regards as the immediate heir of Jean-Jacques and at the same time the first of the socialists, as proving that all the socialist movement of the nineteenth century can be attached directly to the doctrines of Rousseau, but one cannot help feeling that this is to attribute to Fourier a place which he is hardly of sufficient stature to fill. In general terms, one can say that

[1] Espinas, *op. cit.*, p. 91.

the *Discours sur l'inégalité* became, as might have been expected, a more revolutionary work in the hands of the socialists of the next century, but that at bottom Rousseau's ideas involved a recognition of the value of private property for all, which is as difficult to reconcile with the theory of socialism as with the practice of the capitalist state:

3. THE MIDDLE CLASSES

What gives its peculiar quality to Rousseau's social thinking is that, as Taine and Brunetière among others have remarked, he was born of the people, and was never assimilated by the literary world or by the high society he frequented, in which lay his greatest difference from the fashionable writers of whom Voltaire is *par excellence* the type. 'Voltaire,' says Brunetière, 'n'a jamais su ce qui se passe dans l'âme d'un paysan, d'un homme du peuple, d'un laquais, d'une fille d'auberge, ce qu'ils ruminent silencieusement de colères et de haines, ce qui gronde sourdement en eux contre un ordre social dont leurs épaules sentiraient bien encore, à défaut de leur intelligence, qu'ils portent eux seuls tout le poids. Rousseau l'a su, et il l'a su par expérience, et il ne l'a pas dit—il l'aurait plutôt caché, s'il l'avait pu—mais toutes ces rancunes ont passé, pour le grossir et le gonfler, dans le torrent de son éloquence; et Voltaire non plus ne l'a pas dit, mais il l'a bien senti, et qu'il y avait autre chose là-dessous qu'une déclaration d'auteur, et que c'était une déclaration de guerre.'[1]

When Rousseau moved in the fashionable world it was as an alien. He looked at the *noblesse* only to condemn it. 'Mortelle ennemi des loix et de la liberté qu'a-t-elle jamais produit dans la plupart des pays où elle brille, si ce n'est la force de la Tyrannie et l'oppression des peuples.'[2] The cause of his attitude was not, as the cruder type of critic has alleged, that his boorishness brought social failure on him: a good deal of evidence attests his personal charm and his success in the salons of the great. There was something more fundamental in it. Whatever his private feelings, there is in his judgment on society something

[1] F. Brunetière, *Études critiques sur l'histoire de la littérature française*, 3ᵉ série, 1887, p. 277.
[2] *Nouv. Hél.*, ii. 217

of the harshness of the puritan. 'L'élégance lui déplaît,' writes
Taine drastically, 'le luxe l'incommode, la politesse lui semble
un mensonge, la conversation un bavardage, le bon ton une
grimace, la gaité une convention, l'esprit une parade, la science
un charlatanisme, la philosophie une affectation, les mœurs une
pourriture.'[1] In some features at least of this sweeping condemnation there was an element of justice. Despite the charm
of the society that built the Petit Trianon and played at shep-
herds and shepherdesses in the little hamlet of Marie Antoinette,
there was an immense fund of the trivial and worse for the critic
to draw upon. Rousseau, of course, like most other puritan
reformers, condemned indiscriminately the good with the bad.
Moreover certain deficiencies in his mental make-up, notably
his lack of the saving grace of humour, and a singular absence
of appreciation for any of the arts other than literature and
music, prevented him from seeing the more amiable side of the
life of fashionable society.

The obverse of Rousseau's contempt for the *monde* is his
admiration for the people, in which again he is at odds with
Voltaire, for whom the people are *canaille*. For him, on the
other hand, 'C'est le peuple qui compose le genre humain; ce
qui n'est pas peuple est si peu de chose que ce n'est pas la peine
de le compter'. 'Respectez donc,' adds his tutor Emile, 'votre
espèce; songez qu'elle est composée essentiellement de la collection des peuples, que quand tous les Rois et tous les Philosophes
en seraient ôtés, il n'y paraîtraît guère, et que les choses n'en
iraient pas plus mal.'[2] Truly has it been said that there is no
writer more fitted to make the poor proud.[3]

Thus to Rousseau's political democracy we are compelled
apparently to add a demand for social equality in the name of
the people. We have still to ask what Rousseau means when he
talks of the people. It is, for instance, in the mouth of such a
writer as Burke a term of rather limited scope. Similarly, despite
all his democratic sympathies, Rousseau is not to be taken quite
literally. He does not mean by the term 'une populace abrutie
et stupide, échauffée d'abord par d'insupportables vexations,
puis ameutée en secret par des brouillons adroits, revêtus de

[1] H. Taine, *L'ancien régime*, pp. 294-5.
[2] *Œuvres*, iv. 386, 8: *Émile*, IV.
[3] Sainte-Beuve, *Causeries du lundi*, 3rd ed., iii. 79-80.

quelque autorité qu'ils veulent étendre'.[1] Riches and poverty, as has already been said, were alike dangerous to that rule of law which was Rousseau's most dearly held ideal. 'Le riche tient la Loi dans sa bourse, et le pauvre aime mieux du pain que la liberté.'[2]

By its very nature the position Rousseau takes up is one of hostility to extremes. How moderate his practical ideas were is shown by his remarks in the *Constitution de Pologne* or the *Lettres de la Montagne*. As Beaulavon points out, the *Conseil général* of Geneva, which included all the citizens, during the eighteenth century never had more than sixteen hundred members, yet Geneva represents the closest approximation in practice to Rousseau's ideal republic, and he has no idea of increasing the citizen body of Geneva, in praise of whom he writes so eloquently, 'La plus saine partie de la République, la seule qu'on soit assuré ne pouvoir, dans sa conduite, se proposer d'autre objet que le bien de tous'.[3] We do not need to be reminded how Rousseau prided himself that he sprang from that same body, and could sign himself citizen of Geneva. How pathetic, in a sentimental vein, the close of the first book of the *Confessions*, where Rousseau looks back on what might have been his life had he stayed in his native city and pursued an honest craft! For a time the lure of Paris led him to adopt the fashionable habits in which the men of letters aped the aristocracy, but this only makes the more striking his renouncement after his so-called conversion. Of this last we can at least say that it was no mere literary gesture. However worthless his life had seemed previously, from now on his way of living changed. Abandoned were his social ambitions, not — it is only fair to observe — because of lack of success, discarded his gold braid and ornaments, his sword, his white stockings, his fashionable perruque, and in their place he adopted the garb of the lower middle classes. He rejected henceforth the financial help of patrons, renounced the sinecure they had obtained for him and in the end came to earn his living by the pursuit of the only craft he knew, the copying of music. Henceforth he almost overzealously guarded his financial independence. He took Thérèse to live with him

[1] *Pol. Writings*, ii. 283: *Lett. Mont.*, IX.
[2] *id.*
[3] *id.*

and finally went through a ceremony of marriage with her. With a harsh insistence he cut himself off from the world of society, and was content in the last years of his life to sink back into the obscurity of a humble petit-bourgeois existence.

His idea not only of civic, but also of private virtue, is written almost exclusively in terms of middle-class life. The middle classes are for him the salt of the earth. Even when he aims at something more aristocratic, as in his description of the household of Julie and Wolmar, though they own a great estate, and rule their servants and tenants in patriarchal fashion, the existence Rousseau paints is one of simplicity and domestic virtue. Inspired partly by Richardson, himself a eulogist of middle-class life, for whom he had the greatest admiration, Rousseau himself was one channel, says Sainte-Beuve, by which were introduced into French literature the feeling for the home and family and the middle-class virtues which formed so important an element in the ideas of the sentimental school of writers. One might almost argue that the whole sentimental movement in literature was essentially middle class. 'Ces races aristocratiques et fines, douées d'un tact si exquis et d'un sentiment de raillerie si vif, ou n'aimaient pas ces choses simples, ou n'osaient pas le laisser voir. Leur esprit, nous le connaisons du reste et nous en jouissons; mais où est leur cœur? Il faut être bourgeois, et de province, et homme nouveau comme Rousseau, pour se montrer ainsi sujet aux affections du dedans et à la nature.'[1]

In spite of the ridiculous side that there undoubtedly was to sentimentalism, as to the return to nature with which it was closely allied, it sounded the death-knell of the elegant but somehow worthless French society of the eighteenth century. In innumerable ways it revolutionized social ideals; and to a considerable extent even the practices of society were affected by middle-class manners. We find appearing a new simplicity of dress, utilized in revolutionary days as an excuse for fresh extravagances; an only partly serious esteem for manual labour, that made Louis XVI a more successful locksmith than king; a revival of rustic life, with every courtier as a shepherd and every courtesan a shepherdess, the nursing of babies by their own mothers, proud to display publicly their maternal virtues; and

[1] Sainte-Beuve, op. cit., iii. 83.

the rehabilitation of marital fidelity as something more than a sign of eccentricity.

The distinction between the ideals of the middle classes and those of the aristocracy is patent: what needs to be emphasized equally is that Rousseau's standards are all through those of the middle class and not in the least those of the proletariat. All his admiration for the people, all his zeal for democracy, stops dead the moment the limits of the middle class are reached, the moment, that is, that we come to the unpropertied. Some at least of the socialist writers of the nineteenth century have seen this fact and condemned him accordingly. 'En deux mots,' states Proudhon, 'le contrat social, d'après Rousseau, n'est autre chose que l'alliance offensive at défensive de ceux qui possèdent contre ceux qui ne possèdent pas.'[1] He defines it as, 'le code de la tyrannie capitaliste et mercantile'.[2]

This is not entirely fair, it is certainly not the whole truth. Granted that Rousseau's social ideal was the artisan and the small farmer, that he himself at heart always remained a citizen of Geneva, there is a wide gap between this ideal and a social system based on the conjunction of vast wealth on the one hand with an immense proletariat on the other. Rousseau liked neither the over-rich nor the over-poor. Whether it be attributed to his influence or not, in nothing were Robespierre and the Jacobins so much the disciples of Rousseau as in their championship of the small owners of property against both the rich and powerful and the propertyless. When, in the *Lettre à d'Alembert*, he wished to picture an ideal society, it was to his recollection of a district in the neighbourhood of Neuchâtel that Rousseau turned. There, he said, you might see scattered farms, each in the centre of its fields, approximately equal in extent, as were the fortunes of their proprietors, where a prosperous peasantry, immune from taxes and *taille, subdélégués* and *corvées*, cultivating their lands in summer, and in winter occupying themselves in rural handicrafts, were free from the struggles and emulation, as from the temptations of the larger world.[3] With all the defects of character so often attributed to the small owner of property, to have a field, a workshop, a

---

[1] Proudhon, *Œuvres complètes*, ii. 191.

[2] *id.,* ii. 194.

[3] *Œuvres*, vi. 499-500: *Lett. à d'Alembert.*

patch of land and a house of one's own, was a kind of ideal, and one that is not easily rooted out once it has taken hold of a people. 'C'était un rêve, un rêve de Jean-Jacques, sur lequel depuis plus de cent cinquante ans se sont attendries d'innombrables générations de petits gens. "Une maison blanche, avec des contrevents verts. . . . ".'[1]

---

[1] *Le Temps*, April 24, 1933.

CHAPTER VI

JEAN-JACQUES ROUSSEAU AND THE MODERN POLITICAL MIND

1. BACK TO NATURE

Rousseau, I have said, was not a maker of systems: the incompleteness of his political thought is patent. For this reason it is somewhat apt to give an impression of patchwork, of patterns unfinished and threads left loose. I have tried to show that, despite this defect, a fairly consistent scheme of political ideas emerges from his works. There is a kind of unity which results from the activity of a powerful and original mind, dominated by well-defined intellectual preoccupations. That Rousseau's thought possesses such unity becomes manifest above all if we consider his ideas in relation to their basic impulse, the partly intellectual, partly emotional motive force inspiring his political enquiry.

If ever a writer had a single inspiring idea it was Rousseau. His primary interest was ethical. As has often been observed, he was brought by ethics to politics. The apparent impossibility of achieving his ideal for human life and conduct in the existing condition of society convinced him of the necessity for thinking out afresh their political foundations. In order therefore to appreciate the inspiration of his political writings and understand their underlying unity, we must discover what more general principle is hidden behind his political thought. One might suggest that his ideal is freedom. Yet in the *Contrat social* we find the primitive idea of freedom greatly restricted, and in fact natural liberty, as he recognizes, cannot exist once men have agreed to live together in a state. If we reflect on the careful moral training of Emile, the patriarchal *régime* of the *Nouvelle Héloïse*, the civic discipline of the *Contrat social*, the patriotic sacrifices demanded in the *Corsica* and the *Poland*, we can hardly accept the idea of liberty as by itself a sufficient explanation of his political system. Indeed, the note which is sounded throughout Rousseau is the very opposite of unrestrained freedom. His revulsion against tyranny does not lead him to the glorification of anarchy, but rather to the idea of a self-imposed, voluntarily accepted discipline.

For a principle which applies to the fundamental bases of individual psychology we have to turn to the idea of nature. Burke's criticism of metaphysical politicians, that, 'they are so taken up with the rights of man that they have totally forgotten his nature', is precisely that which is least applicable to Rousseau, who in fact is not particularly concerned with the rights of man, but is obsessed with the idea of following nature, included in which of course is human nature. The idea of Natural Man provided his original inspiration, and it is certainly his most persistently reiterated principle. Of course, it was not peculiar to Rousseau, nor was the role it played in his thought fundamentally different from that which it occupied in the intellectual scheme of the whole Enlightenment. This was so important that something more needs to be said of it.

The image of Natural Man is now remembered as one of those illusions which our more enlightened century has outgrown, though ghostly reminiscences still sketch themselves faintly on the literary imagination. In the eighteenth century Natural Man was primarily the noble savage, *Arlequin sauvage*, the simple and virtuous Huron, shocked at the nevertheless fascinating spectacle of the corruptions of civilization, like the noble Red Indians of Jamaica, saving Polly's virtue, wonderfully resurrected after the Beggar's Opera, from the onslaught of civilized pirates and planters. Even the abbé Prévost yielded sufficiently to prevailing taste to introduce the regulation noble savages into his *Histoire de M. Cleveland,* though the author of *Manon Lescaut* must have understood human nature better than to believe in them. This was light-weight stuff, a literary fashion not even reflected in the plastic arts of the eighteenth century. Whatever the destination, Cythera or elsewhere, of Watteau's courtiers and shepherdesses, it was not the State of Nature; Reynolds and Raeburn did not paint Natural Man in a full-bottomed wig, or Boucher and Fragonard natural woman in crinolined and ribboned array or disarray. The art of the Renaissance might seem less remote from nature, but here literature gives us pause. The Renaissance could produce wild men like Caliban, but these are little to our purpose. It is true that

Rabelais set up as an ideal Nature—Physis, the mother of beauty
and harmony, against Antiphysis, which 'by the testimony of
brute beasts drew all the witless herd and mob of fools into her
opinion';[1] but his Natural Man was the ideal inmate of the
Abbey of Theleme, his motto *Fay ce que vouldras.* And this is
'because men that are free, well-born, well-bred and conversant
in honest companies, have naturally an instinct and spur that
prompteth them into virtuous actions and withdraws them from
vice'.[2] Rabelais' Natural Man, in fact, reminds us of Rousseau's
and represents an ideal taken not from nature but from the
classics.

From the Renaissance, therefore, the quest for the source of
Rousseau's Natural Man leads straight back to the Greek idea
of nature. It was, for the Greeks, a process of growth or development, from the seed to the flower, from the beginning to the
ideal end. The ancient world, however, bequeathed also a
different definition of nature. Greek *physis* became Latin *natura.*[3]
This was a change from a philosophical to a legal, and from a
dynamic to a static conception. Nature was now what was in
the beginning; Natural Man was original, primitive, unevolved,
unchanged. His literary representation, in the bucolic idyll of
the Augustans, was the innocent shepherd, ignorant of the
corruptions of the city, obviously the ancestor of the noble
savage. The Latin idea of nature also enshrined the ancient
belief in degeneration, in the tendency of all things to run
down. Nature was for Latin thought not an end but a beginning.
Natural Man was no longer, as for the Greeks, an ideal conception of the highest capacity of man, but a reflection of the
nostalgia of a corrupt civilization for an imagined state of primitive innocence.

It was a long way from these two images of nature in the
ancient world to Natural Man of the eighteenth century, and
they were destined to strange aberrations on the way. The end
of the ancient world was accompanied by the first fundamental
transformation. The Christian philosophy of history incorporated, in the story of the Garden of Eden, a sort of original

[1] *Pantagruel,* Bk. 4, Ch. xxxii. The translation seems to represent fairly well
the sense of the original French.

[2] *Gargantua,* Ch. lvii.

[3] cf. J. L. Myres, *The Political Ideas of the Greeks,* 1927.

State of Nature, and provided in Adam a pastoral image of Natural Man, ignorant of sin or evil. But a second image, not so much superimposed on as replacing this one, was that of Adam and Eve after the Fall, fleeing the wrath of a Jehovah more terrible and implacable than the Furies, toiling, weeping, conceiving in sin, bearing in pain, suffering, dying, in the end murdering; and henceforth the life of man was nasty, brutish and short.

For Christianity there were thus two contrasting ideas of Natural Man, before and after the Fall, which is clearly the central and decisive factor of the new phase in the history of the idea. The Fall, product of man's first disobedience and the fruit of that forbidden tree, the origin of and the Original Sin, is a somewhat mysterious conception: the author of the Old Testament refrained from going into the details that a contemporary writer would regard as essential. However, the idea of Original Sin seems to have been derived, chiefly by St. Paul, not so much from Genesis as from other sources. Perhaps this is why the Early Fathers were rather shaky on the Fall. Irenaeus laid his emphasis on free will and was regrettably ignorant of the inherited corruption of human nature. Clement regarded the pleasure-seeking which leads men to sin as a deliberate act and not congenital. Origen even alleged that the whole Fall story was an allegory. Reason, he said, enables men to choose between good and evil, sin is the result of nurture rather than nature. This, even in its implied contradiction, was frightfully eighteenth century. Pelagius, perhaps with a British inability to appreciate the finer points of religion, even held that human nature is sufficient for a life of virtue, and sin a fault not of man's nature but of his will. All this was most deplorable. One can't tell where it might have ended. In the nick of time St. Augustine came to the rescue of Original Sin: indeed, after St. Paul he may be said to have invented it. For him, human nature was tainted by an hereditary, inborn corruption, and he at least tells us clearly what Original Sin is: it is sex, chiefly as embodied in woman. After this, if not before, there were to be such implications in the ideas of nature and Natural Man right through their history.

The Middle Ages had little doubt that if God created man, the devil had more to do with woman. Natural Man might still have been good if it had not been for Natural Woman. He could not become so again until that source of evil had been transformed. This was a slow process. Passing over the next thousand years we come to the later Middle Ages, when western civilization, at least in its secular shape, began to weaken on the subject of woman. Romances, troubadours, chivalry, pastorals, lyric poetry, all contributed to a less unfavourable picture of the fatal sex. Even religion was tacitly changing its attitude. Female saints were breaking into what had previously been largely a male monopoly and the cult of the Virgin was growing in popularity and intensity. The bucolic or pastoral idyll, which also now reappeared, was not unconnected with the early Christian image of the good shepherd, but the pastoral virtue of innocence implied an irreligious absence of the sense of sin. The reason for the great vitality of the pastoral idyll, indeed, Huizinga has said, was its basically erotic character.[1] The rehabilitation of woman in the later Middle Ages and the Renaissance was evidence of the undermining of the idea of Original Sin, perhaps partly by a revived Aristotelianism which made it difficult to see man as by nature inherently corrupt. In spite of the Augustinianism of the Reformation and the Puritanism of the Counter-reformation, the emancipation of Natural Man from Original Sin survived in secular thought; and in due course it led to the image of Natural Man with which we started—the noble savage of eighteenth-century literature.

Yet a superficial literary fashion such as this would hardly be worth discussing if it were not also something more. The important fact is that the new idea of Natural Man appeared in what was a new world of ideas. It was one element in that moral and intellectual revolution which was summed up by Paul Hazard as the crisis of the European conscience. The new age was dominated by the twin forces of rationalism and individualism, and in this intellectual climate Natural Man was destined to become something of far greater significance than the famous but rather boring noble savage. For the more serious thought of the eighteenth century, Natural Man was the rational, ethical individual, a being of reason and not of history, belonging to a

[1] J. Huizinga, 'Historical Ideals of Life', *Men and Ideas*, 1960, p. 85. (From Huizinga's inaugural lecture 'Over historische levensidealen', 1915.)

K

State of Nature which had ceased to be an historical Eden for an actual Adam, and had become the hypothetical setting of an abstract man. Nature had become a device for isolating the rational individual from society, history and all extraneous influences, and employing this abstraction as a starting-point for the discussion of ethics, religion and politics.

Now, since the eighteenth-century pattern of thought, in spite of all changes, is still the basis of the fundamental ideals of western civilization, its use of the idea of Natural Man in this sense is not only of historical interest but has relevance to our own day and age. Its most important influence on subsequent thought is to be found, perhaps, in the assumption of the identity in basic constitution of the whole human race. The unity of mankind, in a fundamental sense, is an idea as old as Stoic philosophy, but the drawing of practical conclusions had largely to wait until the eighteenth century. The idea of human equality *sub specie aeternitatis* was adopted by Christianity; but not until the eighteenth century was it secularized and brought into relation with the conditions of actual life, and this was achieved by means of the idea of Natural Man. In this way new ethical judgments took shape and were enabled to carry conviction.

Taken as a fact of historical experience, the idea of human equality can easily be shown to be simple nonsense, and it often has been. But of course ethical judgments are not based on historical facts. At the same time, they are nothing at all unless they are susceptible of practical conclusions, and this means bringing them somehow into relation with the realm of practice. The reason why the eighteenth-century Enlightenment was able to develop such an intense concern for ethical values was its equally strong interest in the practical life. Its ethical judgments were put into practice in the form of a host of practical reforms that were then initiated. Yet, while these practical interests were an essential ingredient in the making of a great reforming age, they also presented a major intellectual difficulty. Along with ethical speculation went a positivistic—scientific and historical—respect for actual empirical facts. The problem for the Enlightenment lay in the attempt to reconcile its ethical and its empirical trends. To take an example, if Natural Man were the rational, isolated being of generalized thought, and if he were assumed to be good, it followed, so John Locke, the greatest of the Founding Fathers of the Enlightenment, held, that morals were part of the nature of man. They were a set of rules of universal application, prior to society and laws, equally capable of being deduced by natural reason or observed in natural men, and for a time facts apparently conformed to theory. Under the influence of Molinist ideas of grace and redemption, which challenged the Augustinian theory of Original Sin, the Jesuit missionaries published accounts which seemed to provide a factual basis for the goodness of Natural Man. Subsequent travellers produced a different picture. The things they discovered gave the *philosophes* a *frisson* of rather alarmed pleasure, for the habits of the unspoiled savage were less reconcilable with the traditional ideas of rational and virtuous Natural Man than had been supposed. At the same time the uniformity of the ideal found itself in conflict with the variety of human behaviour.

The lesser writers of the eighteenth century avoided these unpalatable contradictions: they shut their eyes to the facts and persisted in an abstract Cartesian approach to the problem of social morality. The dilemma of Natural Man was admitted more freely by the greater thinkers. Montesquieu, combining an intense interest in empirical facts with a profound belief in the rule of universal law, was torn between a rational and an historical or sociological analysis. He recognized the conflict between nature and ethics. Proclaiming, for instance, that slavery is against nature, he then adds that in some countries there is a natural reason for it. We can see more clearly in Montesquieu than in any of his contemporaries the ambiguity of the eighteenth-century idea of Natural Man: it is the way man lives, but it is also the way in which he ought to live. 'I do not justify customs,' says Montesquieu, 'I give reasons thereof.'

But the Enlightenment was incurably moral: it was not satisfied with what it could not justify. This is what led some—though not the greater thinkers of the Enlightenment—into a superficial optimism. Pope tried to justify the apparent aberrations of nature, including human nature, by man's ignorance of their real purpose.

All Nature is but Art unknown to thee;
All chance direction which thou canst not see;
All discord, harmony not understood;
All partial evil, universal good.

This was to justify nature by the abdication of reason. The greater minds of the Enlightenment were unable to make such a comfortable sacrifice. Bayle, Montesquieu, Voltaire, Diderot, d'Holbach, to name only a few, could not close their eyes to the fact of evil in nature, though they did not account for it by original sin and indeed abandoned the attempt at a theological explanation altogether.

The same dilemma appears in their religious thought. Locke had tried to demonstrate the existence of a natural religion, in the form of a vague, moralistic deism, which he regarded as the product of natural reason. But, with characteristic common sense, he admitted that this natural religion was not adequately 'taken care of' by natural reason. 'Reason, speaking ever so clearly to the wise and virtuous, had never authority enough to prevail on the multitude.' So, in addition, a religion was needed 'suited to vulgar capacities', which evidently the rational, natural religion was not. The idea of a double standard in religion was developed further by subsequent writers. On the one hand, they believed, there was a secret, monotheistic religion of virtue and love held by the élite, and on the other a gross, popular polytheism. As the empirical tendencies of the eighteenth century became increasingly dominant, the latter came to be seen as the real natural religion; and as more and more became known of the often peculiar religious manifestations of the human race, natural religion came to be less like the religion of Rousseau's Savoyard vicar and more like the Golden Bough. As natural religion increasingly came to reflect historical or anthropological fact, it ceased to be compatible with the ideal of rational and Natural Man.

Natural Man, thus, ceased to be the abstract, rational being of Lockian theory, an idea no longer reconcilable with the apparently limitless variety of empirical fact. But he did not disappear. Natural Man now became an abstract ethical idea, or ideal, a measuring-rod against which the facts of actual behaviour could be tested. Voltaire's Natural Man was Candide, slowly and painfully learning the lesson that all is not for the best in the best of possible worlds; but yet while recognizing hard facts, never abandoning his ideals, or the residuary optimistic belief that life is to be understood and controlled by the processes of rational thought. However, there is a weakness in Candide, one must admit, which reveals a similar weakness of Natural Man in this his final transformation: it is that though a brilliant invention for the exercise of Voltaire's wit and reason, and the demonstration of his ethical principles, he is only an *être de raison*—he does not really exist. In spite of his effort in the *Essai sur les Mœurs* to show the unity of nature beneath the diversity of customs, Voltaire's Natural Man was not actual, while actual man was not, in the traditional sense of the word, natural.

But in the course of the eighteenth century interest shifted from abstract Natural Man to actual human nature, which represented a new and major revolution in thought. Rousseau himself was the greatest influence over this revolution. He is often taken as the writer who steered the modern world out of the calm waters of eighteenth-century rationalism and into the stormy seas of romantic unreason and emotion. Voltaire and the *philosophes* certainly believed that this was what he was doing, and feared his influence accordingly. It was perhaps inevitable, after the paradox of Rousseau's First Discourse, that he should have been identified with the argument that the arts and sciences have corrupted the original goodness of human nature; but in reality his thought moves on entirely different lines from this: I have already said that man in Rousseau's State of Nature is an isolated individual, amoral and unsocial, in fact a not very noble savage, yet innocent and not tainted with Original Sin. What he has is 'la faculté de se perfectionner', a latent capacity for reason and morality. When Providence, by its own ways, has forced him into social life, he is faced with new problems. His 'bonté naturelle', innate from the beginning, is no longer adequate to protect him and his fellows from the results of their own passions. He requires a new and a social morality, or virtue. This, in the words of Rousseau, is the triumph of reason over the passions. *Emile* and the *Nouvelle Héloïse* demonstrate the nature of virtue in the individual; the *Contrat social* tries to show how it could be made to operate in society.

Yet there is also foreshadowed, not in Rousseau but in other writers of the period, the opposite conception of Natural Man, inherent in its Jekyll and Hyde history—the brute being of unreason, the Caliban nature revealed by the rising spirit of empiricism and reaction against rationalism. The true nature of man, wrote Vauvenargues in 1741, is in the passions not the reason.

Diderot, perhaps the most forward-looking mind of the Enlightenment, sketched what he called the true story of our wretchedness: once there existed a natural man; there has been introduced into him an artificial man, and in the conflict between the two the poor wretch is racked and torn to pieces. Diderot was arguing, though not wholeheartedly, against the futility of a morality contrary to the facts of nature. Values were evidently changing. As early as 1739 Hume told those, if any, who then read him, 'Reason is, and ought only to be, the slave of the passions, and can never pretend to any other office than to serve and obey them'. And in 1748 Toussaint in *Les Mœurs* proclaimed, 'It is our passions which are innocent and our reason which is guilty', creating an opposition where Rousseau still insisted optimistically there was none.

The new developments that came with the end of the eighteenth century were to push this tendency much farther. There was a reversal of ethical values. The hero and heroine of *Les Liaisons dangereuses* were still rational, but they found that rational happiness lay in doing evil. Rétif de la Bretonne, as he showed in *La Vie de mon Père*, was capable of writing in a pastoral vein; but his peasant was by preference a *paysan perverti*. The precise oddities of perversion do not matter much: the point is that the pleasure lay in the belief that they were perversions. Empiricism had now undermined ethical universality: the individual became a law to himself. Where, for the Enlightenment, to be natural and rational had been to be virtuous, the marquis de Sade made a lunatic pursuit of vice the only natural and reasonable mode of behaviour. Finally, in the German romantic movement Natural Man, a simple creature of instinct, the unthinking member of the herd, the tribal warrior with all the nasty habits of his kind, rejected reasoning altogether. The primitive now replaced the pastoral and Natural Man as an ethical ideal disappeared from the European consciousness, or survived only as an historical Aunt Sally for the shots of the wittier historians of thought.

Natural Man of the Enlightenment was not this. He was, it can be seen, after that way of thinking has been lost, not the noble savage or the simple-minded shepherd, but a device for asserting the potential rationality and goodness of human nature, a means of expressing an ethical ideal. Looking back over this long evolution, which has been sketched so briefly here, we can see that the idea of nature was for Rousseau what it had been for the Greeks, a way of maintaining an ideal of human nature. The abandonment of this idea of nature, the identification of the natural with the primitive—not the ideal primitive of pastoral imagination, but the actual primitive of anthropological investigation—was therefore something more than the end of an illusion. To suggest that such an artificial idea as that of Natural Man, as well as the equally abstract idea of nature that went with it, may have been connected not merely with particular ethical ideas, but with the very survival of ethical thought, or that when rational thinking of the kind that was associated with the ideas of Natural Man and nature was abandoned, ethical judgment went with it, may seem far-fetched. Yet historically it is not unjustified. There is an ambiguity in Rousseau's use of the term nature, as there is for the whole eighteenth century. On the one hand it is the primitive state from which man is rescued by the social contract, and which having been surpassed can never return; but on the other hand it is the conception of nature as an ethical ideal. For this Rousseau more than any other was responsible. He it was who made the idea of nature the ethical, political and critical inspiration of a whole generation.

Rousseau's history of the progress of inequality is the history of the consequence of the abandonment of the ethical ideal of nature. When *amour de soi*, the natural instinct of self-preservation, gives way to *amour-propre*—that sentiment which only allows us to be happy in so far as we are in one way or another better off than our neighbours[1]—the degeneration of natural man, his breaking away from the rule of nature, has commenced; from this comes inequality — not the natural inequality of the stronger over the weaker, but the artificial

[1] Œuvres, xi. 22: Rousseau juge de Jean-Jacques, Première Dialogue.

and functionless inequality resulting from social institutions which create artificial advantages of wealth and birth. These are perpetuated and intensified from generation to generation. Society once established on a false principle, the evil manifests itself in every phase of its activity. Pride and emulation become its motive forces. Instead of a life lived in peace and harmony there is a constant struggle of individuals, each attempting to get the better of his neighbours. The object of life becomes the acquisition and display of wealth and power, and the attempt always to outstrip one's fellows in ostentation is the ruin of all good taste. Simple comfort becomes a sign of social inferiority. Honest morals and natural courtesy are sacrificed to an artificial and meaningless code of politeness. The life of the country is despised and the situation of a worthless lacquey or a penniless courtier preferred to that of the peasant or the country gentleman. And as society becomes more and more complicated and artificial, all natural pleasure is lost, and the ultimate result of the dominance of *amour propre* is the absolute reverse of that maximization of happiness which is the end of utilitarianism.

Rousseau himself is a utilitarian even if with a difference, because he has a different idea of what constitutes human happiness, in other words, to return to the point from which I started, a different conception of human nature. His argument against utilitarianism as a complete explanation of political life is, to put it briefly, that men, corrupted by self-pride and evil institutions, do not obey its principles. 'Presque tous les hommes,' he writes to the elder Mirabeau, 'connaissent leurs vrais intérêts, et ne les suivent pas mieux pour cela'.[1]

The 'return to nature' thus involved a rejection both of the psychological ideas of the *philosophes,* and of the prevailing code of social behaviour. One motive to which has been attributed Rousseau's criticism of society and its institutions is the feeling that all social ties confine and pervert the natural man, but this is the view only of his more pessimistic or paradoxical moments. Certainly he finds a hidden opposition between the constitution of man and that of the societies in which he lives.[2] His deeply rooted personal conviction that human psychology is not well adapted to find contentment in the complicated

[1] *Pol. Writings,* ii. 160: *Lett. à Mirabeau,* July 26, 1767.
[2] *Œuvres,* xi. 238: *Rousseau juge de Jean-Jacques, Second Dialogue.*

civilization of the great state and under conditions of life that can truly be called unnatural, is not patently untrue. But no one who believed that society was in the nature of things bound to be corrupt could have written the *Contrat social* or the latter part of the *Nouvelle Héloïse*. To have denied at least the bare possibility of some approximation to the ideal society of which he dreamed would have driven him to despair. What he says of the evil effects of society on the natural man, for instance in the *Emile*, we must take most often as a criticism of the society of his own day. 'Back to nature' does not mean the abolition of society or a return to the life of the savage prowling shelterless about the woods and living on acorns—Rousseau was too fond of his comfort for that. 'Comment savez-vous,' he wrote indignantly, 'que j'irais vivre dans les bois si ma santé me le permettait, plutôt que parmi mes concitoyens, pour lesquels vous connaissez ma tendresse? . . . Le sage même, s'il en est, n'ira pas aujourd'hui chercher le bonheur au fond d'un désert'.[1] If the misanthropical strain grew stronger in him in his last years, that is to be attributed to his mental troubles and the persecution which drove a sensitive and unstable mind across the borders of sanity, rather to any condemnation on principle of social life. On the other hand it does not seem to me correct to go to the other extreme and link Rousseau's return to nature with the idea of perfectibility instead of primitivism: the idea of progress is one which certainly cannot be attributed to him.

There is, in the last resort, only one way of interpreting the idea of nature as a basic principle of Rousseau's thought. The actual objective existence of the state of nature concerns him not at all; he finds its reality in the mind of man, for its essential principles are 'gravés en nous en caractères ineffaçables'.[2] When he invokes the return to nature he implies on the one hand that there is a certain permanent set of instincts or tendencies which can be called human nature, and which are capable of harmonious development, and on the other hand that human nature is constructed for a certain kind of environment, comprising in the main a simple agricultural existence. There is further implied the judgment that the development of human nature in its appropriate environment and unperverted by evil

[1] *Lettre à M. Philopolis*, 1755.
[2] cf. F. Vial: *La doctrine d'éducation de J.-J. Rousseau*, 1920, pp. 60-6.

institutions is in the nature of things good. Thus the conception of natural man provides Rousseau with an ideal, a standard by which to measure social and political institutions. I have already mentioned some of the practical conclusions as to the good life which he draws, particularly in the economic field. But it is when we go to the root of the matter that we find why the ideal of the return to nature affected so intimately his whole social and political outlook, and was at the same time the source of the bitterest and most pertinaceous criticism he has had to suffer.

He was fully conscious himself of the significance of the issue he was raising. He takes his stand fairly and squarely with those who believe in instinctive human nature. Man in society, he recognizes, needs a careful moral discipline, such as he provides for Emile, but his training is always directed to the drawing out and harmonious development of innate tendencies. It is education with nature, never against nature. It is easy, of course, to find flaws in Rousseau's argument. The cynic may say that the goodness of human nature is easy to prove on his method: if any element in human character seems bad to him he simply assures us that it is not natural. Again, a natural instinct, we might argue, is no more than an 'inherited tendency to behaviour', neither good nor bad in itself. Rousseau's psychological technique was doubtless rudimentary, but even so one cannot help feeling that perhaps he was more aware of the motions of human nature than many of his contemporaries.

His justification may be put in a different way. We may argue that there are natural tendencies which must be accepted as data by ethics, the function of which is not to attempt the impossible and work against nature, but to discuss the modes of operation of innate tendencies and the goodness or badness of the different ways in which they may work. Thus Rousseau's championship of instinct against rationalism may appear simply as a refusal to argue man out of his fundamental nature, and a readiness to accept the instinctive basis of human psychology. That it does not mean discarding the aid of reason to guide and control the operation of instinct, the whole of the *Emile* is proof. Who is the virtuous man, he asks there; and replies, 'C'est celui qui sait vaincre ses affections. Car alors il suit sa raison, sa conscience, il fait son devoir, il se tient dans l'ordre, et rien ne l'en peut

écarter.' . . . 'Il ne dépend pas de nous d'avoir ou de n'avoir
pas des passions: mais il dépend de nous de régner sur elles.'[1] In
a letter of 1768 he defines vertu as force. To be virtuous, he says,
is not merely to be just, but to be so in triumphing over one's
passions.[2]

As for politics, nowhere, and least of all in the Contrat social,
does he show any sign of leaving them to the mercy of blind
instinct or the passions of the multitude. He might easily be
described as extending the Cartesian system to politics. His
appeal is throughout to reason, and the only plausible charge
against his method is that it is unduly rational. In Rousseau's
theory political institutions are still regarded as the work of the
intelligence, in fact of such sublime intelligence that it is only
to be found embodied in the person of some semi-divine legislator. So far he remains one with Locke and the philosophes and a
rationalist in politics. It is this that exposes him to the criticism
of Morley, a somewhat unexpected champion of the sentimental
in politics, who, echoing Burke's charge, declares that politics
is converted by Rousseau into a 'quasi-mathematical science'.
'Its formulae,' he goes on, 'are deducible by rigorous logic from
a fundamental axiom absolutely independent of time and place.
History and observation are simply irrelevant.'[3] This indictment, which, as has been observed, can only be made even
plausible by concentrating on the Contrat social and neglecting
all the other political writings of Rousseau, is equally applicable
to all writers with any title to be considered political philosophers. Human nature being sufficiently stable for us to attempt
to establish general principles of right and wrong, or good and
evil, in politics, these must be based not, as Morley assumes, on
a complete disregard of the facts, but on observation of the
most relevant of all facts, those of human psychology, observed
in the first place where we have the most intimate knowledge
of it, in ourselves. And the only instrument for making this
investigation is the reason.

But Rousseau, as we have seen, keeps the reason to its task in
discussing political principles. He is under no illusions as to the

[1] Œuvres, xi. 376, 8: Émile, V.
[2] Corr. Gén., xix. 58: January 15, 1769; cf. Œuvres, xi. 230, 286: Rousseau
juge de Jean-Jacques, Second Dialogue.
[3] J. Morley, Rousseau, 1873, ii. 19.

political nature of man. He is aware that man is a fond, foolish creature, and that the wisest legislators have recognized the limitations of the material in which they worked. This was why he believed it was necessary to implant the love of the *patrie* and a knowledge of the duties of citizenship by an emotional appeal in early years, when the cold arguments of the abstract reason have no sway. Yet it is one of his most valuable qualities as a political thinker that while admitting the irrationality of man Rousseau still upholds the ideal of reason in politics. Or, to put it the other way round, that the abstract, rational nature of his fundamental argument in the *Contrat social* does not prevent him from acknowledging the necessary emotional elements in political life. On the whole it is true to say that in the age of utility and reason the emotional ingredients in politics were neglected. For their rehabilitation Rousseau certainly deserves, along with Burke, the credit or the blame. The human understanding, he claims, owes much to the passions, without the aid of which nothing that is really great can be attained.[1] It is an error, he says, to attempt to discriminate between those passions which can be permitted and those which must be forbidden. All are good when one has the mastery over them, and bad when they enslave us.[2]

His statement in the *Emile* on this issue is, it may be claimed, a complete justification for the interpretation which I am putting forward. 'Nos passions,' he writes, 'sont les principaux instruments de notre conservation; c'est donc une entreprise aussi vaine que ridicule de vouloir les détruire; c'est contrôler la nature, c'est réformer l'ouvrage de Dieu. . . . Mais raisonnerait-on bien si, de ce qu'il est dans la nature de l'homme d'avoir des passions, on allait conclure que toutes les passions que nous sentons en nous et que nous voyons dans les autres sont naturelles? Leur source est naturelle, il est vrai; mais mille ruisseaux étrangers l'ont grossie. . . . Nos passions naturelles sont très bornées; elles sont les instruments de notre liberté, elles tendent à nous conserver. Toutes celles qui nous subjuguent et nous détruisent, nous viennent d'ailleurs; la nature ne nous les donne pas, nous nous les approprions à son préjudice.'[3]

---

[1] *Pol. Writings.* i. 150: *Disc. inég.*; ii. 168: *Lettre à Usteri*, 1768.
[2] *Œuvres*, v. 377: *Émile*, V.
[3] *Œuvres*, iv. 359-60: *Émile*, IV.

However abstract or intellectualist his method may seem in the *Contrat social*, Rousseau never ceases to be aware of the basic necessity of establishing satisfactory emotional foundations for political society. As early as the *Economie politique* he had drawn the conclusion that the man without passions would certainly be a very bad citizen:[1] while the essay on the constitution of Poland is one long appeal for the bringing in of the motive force of passion to save the state. 'Back to nature', in so far as it meant 'back to human nature', was by no means an unprofitable starting-point for a new school of political thought, nor was the new spirit it introduced unneeded. That Rousseau should himself have been able to produce a complete and final explanation of the psychological foundations of politics was hardly to be expected. It is rather to be wondered at that he was able to comprehend so much of 'human nature in politics' as he did.

By indicating the contrast between man's nature and his highly complicated civilized environment Rousseau diagnosed one of the greatest problems of civilization. His own solution was not, as is often alleged, to give up the problem as insoluble, and abandon the hope of reconciliation, even though, as we have seen, he detested that side of civilization manifested in the life of the great cities and states, and yearned after the restoration of simpler ways of living. Although society is corrupt, says Rousseau in more optimistic mood, yet a man may live even under the government of a despot comparatively free from individual molestation, and the evil he sees round him will make him love the good. 'O Emile! où est l'homme de bien qui ne doit rien à son pays? Quel qu'il soit, il lui doit ce qu'il y a de plus précieux pour l'homme, la moralité de ses actions et l'amour de la vertu.'[2] He hoped, by the educational methods he described in the *Emile*, by the political institutions for which he provided the theoretical basis in the *Contrat social*, by the economic principles scattered through his works, but especially to be found in the Project for Corsica, and by the civic and national ideals emphasized in the *Lettres de la Montagne* and the *Gouvernement de Pologne*, to show the kind of society in which the man of the state of nature would find himself altered

[1] *Pol. Writings*, i. 255.
[2] *Œuvres*, v. 434: *Émile*, V.

certainly but not nullified, and in place of his lost independence would gain a greater freedom. It is thus, and with this principle firmly in mind, that Rousseau effects the transition from the state of nature to political society, and throughout his political writings its operation is to be traced, giving them at bottom that unity which they are sometimes accused of lacking.

2. THE POLITICAL THEORY OF ROMANTICISM: ROUSSEAU AND BURKE

From the idea of nature it is but a step, in the realm of litera-ture, to the full-blown romantic movement. In politics, too, it may be suggested that the same idea produced a revolution against the prevailing system, and that the new movement so plainly manifest in the literary world was not without a parallel in the realm of political ideas. The division of the world of thought into watertight compartments is an academic conven-tion which finds no justification in actual fact. But, it may fairly be asked, can anything be discovered in the history of political though comparable in scope and momentousness to the great literary movement? Does anything exist which we can call the political theory of romanticism, as a coherent and recognizable set of ideas?

In the first place, it cannot be questioned that the romantic period witnessed a great transformation in political ideas. For proof we have only to compare the state of political theory before it experienced the effect of the romantic movement with its state at the beginning of the nineteenth century. A quota-tion which sums up very well this change may be excused here, as evidence that the development in political theory has not gone unrecognized, and moreover that it is capable of being attributed to the influence of the romantic movement. 'C'est aussi un certain sentiment romantique qui distingue l'absolu-tisme de de Bonald ou de Maistre, de celui d'un Hobbes, la sociologie de Saint-Simon de celle de Condorcet ou de Turgot, l'optimisme hégélien de l'optimisme leibnitzien. Il y a chez un Fichte, un Schelling, un Hegel, un lyrisme de la pensée que l'on rencontrerait rarement avant le XIXe siècle.'[1]

[1] J. Wahl, Review of E. Bréhier's 'Histoire de la philosophie', *Revue de Synthèse*, October 1932, iv. 322.

It should be premised, however, that if I speak of the political theory of romanticism it is not as a school in the sense in which the English utilitarians, the *philosophes*, the physiocrats, or even the German idealists can be so described. We have not to deal with any fairly complete or coherent political doctrine, but rather with a tendency, and one moreover of a general and emotional character, not necessarily bound up with any definite practical proposals, and therefore capable of receiving different and even opposed interpretations. How wide the divergence might be will be realized if we consider that the two greatest of those who can be termed the political theorists of romanticism are Jean-Jacques Rousseau and Edmund Burke. And yet the kinship of the ideas of these two men, apparently so widely divided and even diametrically opposed in traditions, political principles, social ideals and character, is not difficult to demonstrate.

It has been assumed too easily that because Burke denounced Rousseau, because the name of the one was identified with the revolution and that of the other with the counter-revolution, their political principles must necessarily have been opposed; but even a brief survey will show that their political ideals were much closer than one would have supposed. A profound belief in the rule of law, an intense hatred of arbitrary government, fear of violent revolution, belief in the necessity of religion to the state, dislike of cosmopolitanism, consciousness of the force of nationality—these are political principles common to the two great men customarily divided by the gulf of the revolution. Nor can we accept the too facile division that classes Burke as the practical politician and Rousseau as the theorist. Burke is no more immune from the plague of principles that in the eyes of the practical man is apt to beset political thinkers than Rousseau himself. In their idea of the state they each move away from the position of Locke and, though quite independently, arrive at conceptions that approximate to a remarkable degree.

Abandoning Locke's reliance on the idea of the state of nature for his theoretical starting-point, art, says Burke, is man's nature. Surely this, it will be said, is the very antithesis of Rousseau's most devoutly held principle? But though in Rousseau the state of nature seems to play a larger part, though he takes it as man's initial state, it is only in order to abandon it the more explicitly and definitively. Whereas Locke kept his state of nature in a condition of suspended animation, for Rousseau there are no such half measures: once man has left that only partially idyllic but wholly temporary state he is condemned for ever to struggle with the problems of society, to pay the price of social morality with a consciousness of sin and with the agony of internal conflict, until the day when the wheel shall have come full circle and man in the ideal society shall know that complete liberty in which he has only to be himself in order to achieve perfect morality, and so the conflict should be finally over. But this state of perfection, always to be striven for, was never to be attained; and in the meantime man must endure the strife within himself, the road back for ever barred by the angel with the flaming sword, the state of nature for ever lost. One cannot doubt Rousseau's meaning. In the political state he, like Burke, for all practical purposes abandons the conception of the state of nature; and if he begins by asserting the principle of natural rights, it is only to alienate them the more completely once the social contract has been concluded. Burke is here nearer to Locke, because if in general hostile to the idea of natural individual rights he at least admits the possibility of an appeal to them in extreme cases.

The fate of the contractual theory of the state is even more significant. For Burke, man needs no social contract; he is born into society, and can no more exist without it than he can without the air he breathes. Rousseau, if he does not abandon the Lockian idea of contract, at least robs it of its most important ingredient—the free and rational choice of the individuals composing society. Theoretically he allows the individual at the time when he reaches adult status the choice whether he will attach himself politically to the particular community he chances to inhabit. But as to the terms of the contract he allows no choice at all. They are dictated by the unalterable laws of right and wrong. The real distinction here between Rousseau and Burke is that Burke, regarding political constitutions as so many natural phenomena, is prepared to accept all of the various historic forms in which the state is manifested as justified by the test of prescription; whereas Rousseau, in the pursuit of an ideal, is—at least in the *Contrat social*—concerned to discover the nature of the perfect state. Acton says that 'Rousseau's error was in affirming that society comes from Contract. Burke denied that the State itself comes from it—also wrong',[1] but I cannot believe that either Rousseau or Burke was so completely conscious of a distinction between state and society. The political unity was for both the essential characteristic of the unity of society.

For both, too, this political unity, although embodied in a constitution, had its real being not in any institutional forms but in something less concrete, in the consciousness of unity existing in the minds of the citizens, in the feeling of oneness that makes a collection of individuals into a community. Again, for Burke as for Rousseau, the ultimate end of the state was the well-being and happiness of its members. Both admitted in the last resort a certain sanctity attaching to the voice of the people, and by both the 'people' in a political sense was interpreted in a very limited fashion.

Where then comes the cleavage between them? Not in their basic ideas of the state, but rather in the fact that for Rousseau the legislative sovereignty of the general will, so long as it remains general in nature, is unlimited and illimitable. Burke, on the other hand, limits the legislative activity of the state in innumerable ways, by dividing it among subordinate but independent authorities, by subtracting from it the whole sphere of moral and religious life, which is submitted to a rather arbitrarily conceived notion of fundamental law, by refusing even in purely political matters to allow it to interfere, except in the most limited manner, with the work of time, the traditions and the ancient laws and institutions of the country. And hence it is that, despite the close relationship of their primary political conceptions, the theory of Rousseau could be used to justify a revolutionary government of which Burke was the bitterest opponent.

Yet we should be wrong to ignore the fact that there is a conservative hidden in Rousseau, just as there is a revolutionary in Burke. It is as though he himself were afraid of the power he had created, and were concerned to limit, to the utmost of his ability, its scope. There is this curious contradiction in Rousseau, that while he is the author of political principles

[1] *Acton MSS.*, Camb. Univ. Lib., Add. 5401.

L

giving the widest scope to the powers of the sovereign general will he is very reluctant to see these powers exercised. In the *Lettres de la Montagne* he argues that aversion against novelties is generally well founded: the government can hardly put too great an obstacle in their way, for however useful they may appear, the advantages they offer are nearly always less sure than the dangers are great.[1] More unexpectedly, at the beginning of the *Emile* he declares that in the social order the rank of each is laid down, the child must be brought up for the social position he is to occupy as a man.[2] Finally, such a passage as the following is the very echo of Burke: 'Le moindre changement dans les coutumes, fût-il même avantageux à certains égards, tourne toujours au préjudice des mœurs. Car les coutumes sont la morale du peuple, et, dès qu'il cesse de les respecter, il n'a plus de règle que ses passions, ni de frein que les lois, qui peuvent quelquefois contenir les méchants, mais jamais les rendre bons.'[3]

This presents us with an aspect of Rousseau's political theory in which he is closer to the English than to the French tradition. The explanation of the co-existence of extreme principles and conservative practical ideas is that Rousseau has a clear sense, though he does not put it so explicitly as Burke, of the distinction between the right and the possible. Rousseau has at least the courage of his pessimism, that of recognizing the right and yet acknowledging that it may be unattainable. Since he wrote a book which was concerned with what is right almost to the exclusion of what is possible, and was in addition a work of genius, naturally it was seized upon by adherents and opponents alike, while his more moderate practical conclusions were neglected. Nevertheless, as I have tried to show, ample indications are given in Rousseau's works of the extent to which he shared the conservative tendencies characteristic of the romantic movement in politics.

One should note also the source of this conservatism. It is neither based, as was much nineteenth-century conservative political theory, on historical grounds, nor on a desire to leave free scope to evolution and the play of natural forces. History

---

[1] *Pol. Writings*, ii. 239: *Lett. Mont.*, VIII; *cf. id.*, ii. 265: *Lett. Mont.*, IX.
[2] *Œuvres*, ii. 14; *Émile*, I.
[3] *id.*, viii. xxiv: Preface to *Narcisse*.

indeed forms a somewhat doubtful and double-edged weapon, for a historical philosophy can as easily be made the basis of a revolutionary as of a conservative political creed. The conservative political tendencies of the first romantic generation were based on the facts of human nature rather than on theories of history — on a consciousness of the emotional constituents of human nature, of the powerlessness of the isolated individual and of the importance of the community as the sentimental and historical unit that we call in modern times the nation.

Rousseau here, as at so many other points, stands with one foot in either camp. He never outgrew the methods of intellectual analysis of Cartesian logic, or the individualism learned from Locke; but he added to these a belief in nature of a new kind, the nature of the individual man, in all its variety, and the nature of all the individual, local and national variations that complicate problems for the student of society. One cannot but see here a reflection of the literary opposition between classical uniformity and the romantic movement with its preference for the qualities of diversity and strangeness. It cannot be alleged that Rousseau went so far as Burke in the approval of positive abuses merely because they were old or peculiar to a nation. Nevertheless it is clear where his sympathies lie and why, despite his theory of sovereignty, he is to be classed with the conservatively minded Romantics.

The danger in describing a thinker as conservative or revolutionary is that these terms bring with them an almost unavoidable connotation of approval or disapproval, which is irrational, since conservation and revolution are equally necessary and justified in different circumstances, and it all depends on what one wishes to conserve or destroy. In Rousseau the combination of the revolutionary and the conservative is unusually clearly marked, and each element contributed its quota to his political thinking. But since revolution implies change and conservatism repose, his revolutionary principles were a call to action, his conservatism an aid to understanding. Nor is there fundamental schism or conflict between the two sides of his mind. Without the insight into the deeper forces of human nature which is the source of his conservative tendencies, what was really original, what indeed was most truly revolutionary in his political philosophy could never have existed, and Rousseau would have counted as one of the rank and file of the *philosophes* and no more.

3. THE INDIVIDUAL AND THE COMMUNITY

To the end a hard and insoluble core of individualism remains in Rousseau's thought and refuses to be dissolved away by the rising tide of communal values. Even in politics the sacredness of individuality and the importance of the individual initiative is still his guiding principle. To borrow the acute summing-up of Baldensperger — 'Ce point vif du rousseauisme confronté avec le romantisme, il est dans ce que j'appellerai *l'indifférence ou l'hostilité aux intermédiaires* dans la société, dans la religion et dans l'art'.[1] This is why we have to discard Vaughan's description of him as 'the sworn foe not only of individualism, but of individuality'.[2] In another place, indeed, Vaughan is compelled to characterize Rousseau as 'of all those who have pleaded the cause of individual freedom . . . the most passionate and inspired'.[3] We may be sure that Rousseau, for whom in other respects individuality is so precious, would not omit it from his political ideal—all the more because his moral principles are imbued with an intense individualism, possibly Calvinist in inspiration, and because for him politics and ethics are hardly separable. Those who attempt to divide them, he declares,. will never understand anything of either.[4]

For this reason alone he is bound to reject any theory which sinks the individual so completely in the mass as to rob him of his capacity for moral freedom. Even when he exalts the community and appears to demand the sacrifice of the individual, it is because a voluntary identification of the individual with the community of which he is a member seems to him necessary for his moral well-being. But since he starts from the individual and not from the community he envisages the moral end in terms of individuals, and takes all political and social organizations, right up to the national community itself, as at best means, even if necessary ones.

[1] Baldensperger, etc., *J.-J. Rousseau*, 1912, p. 284.
[2] *Pol. Writings*, i. 59.
[3] *id.*, i. 112-13.
[4] *Œuvres*, iv. 408: *Émile*, IV.

Nor is his individualism only a matter of philosophy. In politics Rousseau required that the individual citizen should exercise his judgment in politics, because, as a member of the sovereign, it was his duty to play his part in the determination of the general will of the state. The very existence of the general will is equivalent to laying down a programme for the individual. It necessitates that his judgment shall be rational, in the general interest, and unperverted by selfish prejudices or individual passions. It is not enough for him passively to accept the laws of society. He may be only a unit, but Rousseau intends him to be an active unit in the state, and to take his rights and duties very seriously. Indeed only in the small city state—in which each citizen can in turn take part in the positive functions of government, and all have a direct voice in legislation—can this ideal be fully realized. The *Contrat social* is essentially a theoretical work, but its intention is to expand and not to obliterate individuality in the corporate life of the state.

Rousseau represents, as definitely as Burke, the breakaway from pure Lockian individualism. 'That,' concludes Vaughan, 'is his historical significance. Standing at the parting of the ways, he embodies the results of the past; he prepares the ground for the wholly different ideals of the future.'[1] Locke, Vaughan argues, by making the individual morally sufficient unto himself had divorced politics from ethics. Rousseau, by recognizing the necessity of the community to the individual's moral life, brought ethics and politics again into connection with one another.[2] It is, he says, 'a reversion from the cramped and narrowing view of Locke'.[3] On the one hand this verdict seems to me unduly to depreciate Locke's political thought, and on the other to be over-confident of the value of that conception of a 'higher unity' which was to take its place. Nor, as I have stated already, does it seem to be fair to regard Rousseau's thought merely as a half-way house between two rival theories, a stepping-stone from one extreme to another. On the contrary, the object of his political philosophy is to effect a reconciliation between the individual and the state, in which each may

[1] *Pol. Writings*, i. 4.
[2] *id.*, i. 40, 50-2.
[3] *id.*, i. 113.

acquire a fuller meaning. Only in the light of such an interpretation can we understand his position in the development of political thought, and explain the apparent contradiction by which the assertion of the rights of the individual is joined to the creation of the idea of a more closely integrated state.

Rousseau's individualism has peculiarities of its own, which is why some have unjustly denied its right to the title. It does not leave the individual isolated and defenceless against the state, or against any other organized force. Instead, using as his basis the moral freedom of the individual, Rousseau builds up from it the authority of the community: he makes use of the very forces which tend to absorb the individual in the community for the safeguarding of his independence. The price which he makes the state pay for the right to exercise the sovereignty given by the general will is precisely that which is required for the maintenance of the real liberty of the individual wills themselves; for the sovereignty of the general will in the conditions which he lays down involves the direct creative participation of the individual citizen in making the laws of the state.

As he pictured it such an ideal may be possible only in the small city state. Rousseau may be said to have prophesied the fate of his own ideal, since the larger and the more complicated the state, the farther removed it must necessarily be, he believed, from that ideal. We may ask whether he is not also open to the accusation of being himself a prophet of those tendencies which have proved most fatal to his own principles? If he did not in so many words accept the guidance of sheer sentiment in politics, did he not, by exalting natural instinct and extolling the virtue of the simple unspoiled emotions of the people, prepare the way for government by mob emotion and by the most potent and dangerous of the forces by which the feelings of the masses could be roused and flung into the scales of politics, nationalism and democracy? Are there not grounds for the accusation that he preached the ideals of the sovereign people and the self-sufficient nation; and that having evoked this power he completed his work by embodying it in the state, to which he allowed a sovereignty as absolute as the mind of man could conceive, from the scope of which neither religion nor any other human activity was excluded?

I have attempted earlier to indicate the unfairness of such a summary of Rousseau's political creed. But in history the half-truth is potent: there is a kind of Gresham's law by which moderate ideas are expelled by extreme ones. Rousseau envisaged clearly certain forces — those in particular of democracy and nationality—which were to count for more in the Europe of the future than in that of the past. If he did not create these forces, he helped to precipitate them out of the general current of European thought. Since he ignored the problems presented by the great nation state—hardly a reality in his own day, it is true—he naturally failed to appreciate its dangerous possibilities; and he lauded the national principle more highly than was wise in view of the fact that, as was to be shown in practice, it was to prove of doubtful compatibility with his own liberal and individualistic ideals.

That he was reacting against excessive individualism is as evident as that he was groping towards some kind of fundamental change. Society, as he saw it, was unsatisfactory because ill adapted to human nature. Its institutions were bad because they were artificial, and they were artificial because they were not the necessary product of man and his environment but had been created by the force and cunning of small interested sections of the community; by the selfishness and pride of priests — he agreed so far with the *philosophes*—but added to his indictment kings and nobles and all in authority. Now since man is helpless in the grip of evil institutions, improvement could only come about by a major change, by the replacing of existing institutions with others framed not in the interests of particular classes but appropriate to the well-being of all citizens. It was thus in the interests of the individual that Rousseau put forward his new conception of society.

Given this awareness of the need for new social conceptions, it will be asked, did he not simply react against the old ideas and rush to the opposite extreme? The many relics—to put it no higher—of individualism in his doctrine suggest the contrary. But if not a mere blind reaction, what then was the process by which Rousseau attempted to discover institutions better adapted to human nature? Here, it may be suggested, we can observe a dual trend in his thought. There are two methods of approaching this problem, and in a certain sense they lead to opposed results. In the first place, one can by introspection seek out the essential characteristics of human nature, and subsequently by logical deduction establish the principles of government necessary for the achievement of the good life. Starting from the individual, this method naturally tends to produce individualistic results.

The intrinsic value of Rousseau's analysis of the principles governing social and political relations depends on the soundness of the presuppositions on which it is based — that is to say, primarily on the value of Rousseau's interpretation of human nature in politics. To the more individualistic Rousseau, then, we are forced back once again. He does his best to take man as he is, a being partly rational, partly emotional, influenced by considerations of utility, but even more swayed by passions and prejudices, at bottom moral and virtuous, but easily corrupted by bad institutions, and in most cases dependent for the maintenance of his virtue on good ones. The political analysis on which rests in the last resort the value of Rousseau's political thought, is not completely individualist, while at the same time it is equally not based on any glorification of society as distinct from the individuals of which it is composed.

Rousseau allows to those communal forces of which the reality cannot be questioned their place in the life of society, without sacrificing the individual wholly to them. It was his virtue to have been able to give something like their due to both factors in the social problem, to the individual as well as to the communal aspect. There is here another justification for linking him with the other political theorists of the early romantic movement, with Burke, and with the Lake Poets, who were disciples equally of the English and the French thinker. Their especial merit is that, while maintaining firmly an individualistic ideal, they recognize the necessity of the community to the individual, and the reality and vigour of the emotional life of which it is the centre. This duality in his thought by itself explains why Rousseau, like Burke and the Lake Poets, had no real disciples in political theory, why he founded no school, and remains to the end an isolated thinker, like them denounced by individualists for *étatisme*, and by authoritarians for his individualism.

In conclusion, it can be said that by way of the conception of

the general will Rousseau steps out of the intellectual sphere of
the Natural Law jurists and becomes the spiritual precursor of
the Idealist philosophers. Religion and politics, divorced by the
political thinkers of the seventeenth and eighteenth centuries,
are herein reunited. True, the state in which the general will
prevails is little more than a utopist ideal, and by his rigid distinction between sovereignty and government Rousseau limits
the function of the general will to the establishment of laws. All
the same, in the idea of the general will is to be found the justification for holding that the social contract emancipated the conception of political power from the limitations which had
hitherto encompassed it. Here, also, is the explanation of
Rousseau's somewhat confused language in dealing with Natural
Law. Allowing that, as M. Derathé claims, he does not reject the
idea of Natural Law, at the same time he comes close to identifying it with the general will. In so far as this identification is
assumed it means that the idea of Natural Law ceases to be
capable of playing its former rôle in the state as a moderating
influence over political power. In sum, Rousseau's general will is
an ideal of perfection, in which supreme power is also unqualified liberty, in which reason and sentiment are united, and will
is the same thing as law; it is the belief that there can be a state
in which all passion is silenced by the voice of reason, and, in
the words of Hardy,

. . . deliverance offered from the darts that were,
Consciousness the Will informing, till It fashion all things fair.

It was an entrancing vision, such as had not been offered to
the European mind since the time of Plato. But it was also
dangerous. Natural Law, contract, utility, may have led
Rousseau thus far; now his thought takes wings and leaves them
behind, and with them the foundations of the liberal, individualistic, rational tradition in which he himself had been bred.
The prospect revealed by the *Contrat social* seemed a fair one.
The infusion of a religious spirit into politics offered a way of
escape from the legal formalism of the contractualists and the
mundane concerns of the utilitarians, all the more welcome
because it was a religious spirit untrammeled by the dogmas of
a traditional creed. Rousseau was no philosopher, but he was a
master of philosophers, and Kant discovered in his writings the

M

words which were the open sesame to a new philosophic treasure house. On the other hand, having said so much, it must be added that Rousseau, if he opened the door, did not go through it himself; he did not follow where the spirit led. It is not uncommon for a great discoverer to fail to realize the full implications of his own ideas; and Rousseau could not abandon the ideals he had learned at the feet of the great teachers of Natural Law. If, in the end, one is tempted to link him not with his precursors but with his successors, it must be with the recognition that the heritage he left was one which he would hardly have understood, and almost certainly have disavowed.

Implicit in Rousseau's political thought is the main problem of twentieth-century political life: given the reality of nationalism, state sovereignty, the demand for the enforcement of economic equality by the state, and the emotional basis of popular politics, how to reconcile these with political principles founded on the idea of the rational, self-determining individual, the free citizen, and derived ultimately from Greek ideas of justice and liberty? Rousseau offered no permanent solution; so far as the great state was concerned he thought that none was possible. His attempt, so far as it went, to hold the balance between the individual and the community, as between reason and emotion in politics, may not now be calculated to win favour in political theory. The collapse of divine right and the bankruptcy of hereditary aristocracy may seem to have launched the world on a sea of change in which nothing is permanent. Yet there still remain, unchanged in a changing world, on the one hand, the community and its will to live, and on the other hand the divine spark of individuality in Western civilization, the eternal capacity of the individual for taking the initiative, and the perennial life of the principles of political freedom first enunciated in ancient Greece. Delivered over apparently to the mercy of great communal movements of opinion, unforeseeable and uncontrollable, the individual may have seemed helpless and the ideals that Rousseau upheld mere dreams. Yet, whereas the tide, when this book was first written, was running strongly against them, in some respects at least it has turned, and in the words of the judicious Sainte-Beuve, 'Quand le courant des idées publiques sera aux choses saines et généreuses, la renommée de Jean-Jacques revivra'.

POLITICAL IDEAS OF THE COMTE D'ANTRAIGUES[1]

So much has been made of the influence of Rousseau over the revolutionaries that the example of a royalist, who ended as an *émigré* of a most reactionary type, and yet all through his career claimed to be a disciple of Jean-Jacques, is more worthy of study than the intrinsic value of his ideas would suggest. Moreover, while the influence of Rousseau over the revolutionaries is almost invariably discussed in vague general terms, we can here examine the effect of specific doctrines and ideas. A young provincial noble of the Vivarais, with tolerable revenues, though excluded from the charmed circle of *noblesse de cour*, d'Antraigues, after an early and not very successful attempt at a military career, turned to the more attractive and in the eighteenth century possibly more arduous life of the literary *dilettante*. He moved in the minor literary circles of Paris, stayed with Voltaire, made chemical experiments, was enthusiastic over Montgolfier, fell body and soul under the spell of the worst kind of Rousseauist sentimentalism, and from time to time retreated to his mountain fortress of *La Bastide*, there to deliver himself over to a debauch of literary composition in the romantic *genre*. He has some title to be considered not merely as a disciple of Rousseau, but as—in political theory—his first disciple. According to his own statements he was personally acquainted with Rousseau in the last years of his life, and even if d'Antraigues exaggerated the extent of their acquaintance there is sufficient evidence to make it highly probable that it was not entirely fictitious. At any rate he was clearly a convinced Rousseauist in the early 'eighties, and like many others produced a series of literary efforts in the style of his master, which were destined to remain in manuscript, but which serve to show that even so early he had become initiated into the political ideology of Rousseau.[2] When in 1789 a critic accused him of having been seduced by the ideas of Rousseau, he proudly replied, 'Ah! I may well hope that the

[1] For the life of d'Antraigues see L. Pingaud, *Un agent secret sous la Révolution et l'Empire: Le comte d'Antraigues*, 1895.

[2] A selection of letters from the d'Antraigues MSS., purporting to be by Rousseau, was published, with a commentary by A. Cobban and R. S. Elmes, under the heading, 'A disciple of Jean-Jacques Rousseau: the comte d'Antraigues'. *Revue d'histoire littéraire de la France*, vol. 43, pp. 181-210, 340-63.

ideas of that great man have become my own. . . . If to unite in the same heart and for the same object the most perfect esteem, the greatest respect, a friendship which only death could end, cruel and lovely remembrances which make his memory the torment and the charm of my life, if to unite all these sentiments is a proof that I have been seduced by his principles, then certainly I am guilty and will never cease to be so.'[1]

We find in d'Antraigues' writings a mass of general phrases culled from Rousseau. Man is born free; in the state of nature, 'far from the fetters of society, in wild and savage regions', he preserved his native independence.[2] Though he may since have forsaken the state of nature, the immutable rules of natural and divine justice have been implanted in his heart, and these remain when despotism has destroyed all other relics of his natural liberty. To these principles men may appeal in the last resort, and rediscover in them the sacred rights of the people.[3] This provides the theoretic argument on which d'Antraigues based the book through which—because of its opportune appearance, the nature of its appeal, some happy phrases, and the fact that its author belonged to the *noblesse*—he achieved an all too evanescent popularity and fame. In commencing with the natural rights of the people d'Antraigues provides a very clear example of the popular interpretation of Rousseau's ideas. By the immutable law of nature, he says, it is the people by and for which the state exists: its interest must be the supreme interest in the state and its will the supreme will.[4] Nor was he afraid to repeat the same principle, which indeed by then the rest of the world was equally proclaiming, before his fellow nobles in the National Assembly. The essential principle, he said, with typical redundance, is that 'All authority resides in the people; all authority comes from the people; all legitimate power emanates from the people'.[5]

D'Antraigues joined to the argument based on the natural rights of the people an argument of a different order, that in fact popularized by the adherents of the *Parlements*, particularly after 1771, and derived from the medieval constitution of France. The connection between the idea of the state of nature and this more historical theory is provided by the semi-legendary age of the Franks, when, 'Gathered together in the *Champs de Mars* around a king whom the

[1] d'Antraigues, *Supplément au Mémoire sur les États de Languedoc*, 1789, pp. xvii-xviii.

[2] *Mémoire sur les États Généraux*, 1788, p. 8.

[3] *id.*

[4] *id.*, pp. 198, 246.

[5] *Discours sur la Sanction Royale, prononcé dans l'Assemblée Nationale*, 1789, p. 2.

people had elected, the general will dictated the law'.[1] But when the free Franks became rulers of the subject Gauls, the decline of liberty began, fiefs became hereditary and feudalism, the rule of anarchic violence, was born. In search of protection the people turned to the king, who called the *états généraux*, of which, though the nobles and the clergy each had their separate estates, the *tiers état*, the representative of the people, was the essence. One can understand why in 1788 a work should attain popularity in which the *tiers état* was invoked as, 'the body most worthy of respect, that in which all power really resides, that which alone sustains the state, and which is really the nation itself, while the others are only subordinate'.[2]

But to the careful reader, even in this his first work the more conservative tendencies of d'Antraigues will be evident, and what is particularly interesting is the extent to which they also can be associated with principles derived from Rousseau. The most important of these, on account both of the frequency with which he reiterated it and the consequences it was to involve in the realm of practical politics—the all-important qualification, indeed, which was bound to bring him into the ranks of the counter-revolutionaries— was the principle that the general will cannot be represented.[3] He concluded that though in a state of any size representation is inevitable, the representatives must be kept strictly within their proper limits and not allowed to arrogate to themselves that legislative sovereignty which belongs only to the people. The tyranny of one man, he said, introducing an argument that was to be echoed many times after, is preferable to that of twelve hundred deputies.[4] 'In a great empire democratic government is the cruellest of all despotisms.'[5] He supports his position by citations from the *Contrat social* and the *Constitution de Pologne*.[6] It is interesting to note that d'Antraigues is fully aware that, though based apparently on an extremely democratic idea, this is really a conservative principle. He describes it as 'this conservative principle, that our deputies to the *états généraux* are not appointed to decide the destiny of the state. that they are no more than simple mandatories, . . . and that in no case and on no pretext may they diverge from the instructions which they have received'.[7] To this principle of *mandats impératifs*, and as

[1] *Mémoire sur les États Généraux*, p. 10.
[2] id., p. 93.
[3] id., p. 234.
[4] *Quelle est la situation de l'Assemblée Nationale*, 1790, p. 29.
[5] id., p. 11.
[6] *Supplément au Mémoire sur les États de Languedoc*, pp. xviii, xix.
[7] *Mémoire sur les États Généraux*, p. 125.

well as frequent incidental references in his many political pamphlets, he expressly devoted a *Mémoire*.[1]

The rejection of the representative system leads, except in the tiniest of states, to an *impasse*. We have already seen that in order to escape from this difficulty Rousseau proposes the system of a federation of small republics; and it affords confirmation of this interpretation that in d'Antraigues the same suggestion is put forward for precisely the same reason, with definite reference to Rousseau. But d'Antraigues only mentions the idea to reject it, not on theoretic grounds, but because he regards it as mere utopism, forbidden in France by the circumstances of the country and the character of the people.[2] At the commencement of the revolution, it seemed to him, the principle was being used as a means of undermining the authority of the crown, and this was the excuse he gave for the destruction of a manuscript fragment by Rousseau on *républics confédératifs* that he alleges himself to have possessed.[3] D'Antraigues' revolutionary ardour did not go very far in practice. He could find ample support in Rousseau for believing that in a large state such as France monarchy was a necessity. Even in the *Mémoire sur les États généraux* he expresses this view, which the early events of the revolution only served to accentuate. To begin with he presents the authority of the king primarily as a means of safeguarding the liberty of the people, by imposing a check on the representatives.[4] But by 1790 he is allowing the monarchy more positive functions. 'The extensiveness of the realm, the indestructible will of the people to form but a single state, its horror of the division of the monarchy into confederated republics, necessitate a common centre in which may be united all the threads of government.'[5]

After his emigration d'Antraigues' ideas enter a third phase. Though counting, of course, as a royalist, and for a short while ranking high in the councils of the *émigrés*, he now lays a diminished emphasis on the rights of the crown. Like many other nobles, while the king was in the hands of the revolutionaries he declined to recognize him as a free agent, and the rights of the *noblesse* came to occupy the key position in his political system, formerly held by the idea of the sovereignty of the people. Not until 1792 does this appear clearly, however. In this year he printed his *Addresse à l'ordre de la*

---

[1] *Mémoire sur les Mandats impératifs*, 1789.

[2] À *l'Ordre de la Noblesse du Bas-Vivarais*, 1789, pp. 51-2 n.; *Discours sur la Sanction Royale*, p. 14 n.; *Quelle est la situation de l'Assemblée Nationale?* pp. 31-3.

[3] *Quelle est la situation . . . , p.* 59 n.

[4] *Discours sur la Sanction Royale*, p. 5.

[5] *Quelle est la situation . . . , p.* 16.

noblesse de France (written in November 1791), in which he begins by recanting the distinction he had formerly made great play with, between the *noblesse* of the court and the *noblesse* of the provinces. This division, he says, was the work of those who planned to destroy the monarchy by first destroying the *noblesse*. In defence of his own order he waxes increasingly enthusiastic. It is now the *noblesse* and no longer the *tiers état* which is 'le plus beau domaine du peuple', and which exists by and for the people.[1] Its privileges he brushes aside as being mostly nominal and at any rate quite harmless. Distinctions of rank and inequalities of wealth are necessary to the social order, he maintains, because nature has distributed ability unequally, and it is right that those who are '*l'élite de la nation*' should form a superior order.[2]

Even the *Parlements* share in the rehabilitation of the *ancien régime* in his esteem.[3] In place of rhapsodies on the *tiers état* we now have continual denunciations of democracy, justified still—so strong was the hold of Rousseau over him—by the declaration in the *Contrat social* that pure democracy is the worst of all forms of sovereignty.[4] But by 1792 the *Contrat social* has become for the disciple of Jean-Jacques no more than 'the romance of a great genius, who, finding only corrupt men on earth, populated a new universe with his chimeras, and legislated for the men whom his imagination had created'.[5] The sovereignty of the people he describes a few years later as a 'droit chimérique'.[6] As for the *tiers état*, what is left when the superior orders are taken away from the state is not the people but a mere rabble. 'It is a class,' he writes, with characteristic arrogance, 'of which a great part lives at the expense of all those who are superior to it, and towards which the state is more than just if it accords it the same rights as to the other classes.'[7] But although his expressions were now more violent, so far as his criticism of democracy went he had held the same view even in the early part of 1789. Democracy in a great empire, he had written then, is anarchy. 'The reign of anarchy is short; out of the horror which it inspires is born the desire for order and the love of peace; and thus despotism reappears.'[8]

[1] *Addresse à l'ordre de la noblesse de France*, 1792, p. 93.
[2] *Réponse du comte d'Antraigues à l'Auteur constitutionnel du Coup d'œil sur la Révolution française*, 1795, pp. 96-7, 128.
[3] *Exposé de notre antique et seule légale Constitution*, 1792, pp. 49, 56.
[4] *Lettre . . . à MM . . . , Commissaires de la Noblesse de B . . .* , 1792, p. 9 n.
[5] *Addresse à l'ordre de la noblesse de France*, p. 102 n.
[6] *Réponse . . . à l'Auteur constitutionnel*, etc., p. 152 n.
[7] id., etc., p. 100.
[8] *Troisième Discours prononcé dans la Chambre de la Noblesse*, 1789, p. 12.

His defence of the privileges of the *noblesse* and his attacks on democracy are easily comprehensible but of little value. It is more interesting, however, to find in him also the beginnings of a generalized conservative philosophy, the arguments for which he derives, at least in part, from Rousseau's *Gouvernement de Pologne*. The *Contrat social*, he says, is an isolated and abstract work, not applicable to any actual state. Rousseau, on the other hand, when he had to apply his principles to an already existing nation, 'at once modified his principles in accordance with the ancient institutions of the people, allowing for all prejudices too deeply rooted to be destroyed without injury to the fabric of the state'.[1] Rousseau's nationalism is clearly one source of d'Antraigues' conservatism. 'Just as with individuals, one can observe even in the earliest age of a nation the traits which compose its national character, . . . and it is as a consequence of this that a constitution which is practicable for one nation is often detestable to another, because it is repugnant to its national character. The result is that the best of all constitutions for a nation is certainly that which it has received from its ancestors, and which has been successively enlarged and modified by its fathers.'[2] He concludes elsewhere that the constitution cannot be changed without the agreement of all classes in the state, because it is connected necessarily in all parts with the manners, character, climate and general circumstances out of which it has grown.[3]

In respect of these ideas, however minor a luminary, d'Antraigues is clearly to be placed in that romantic galaxy of which Burke and Rousseau are the great though opposed stars. This is made the more evident by another element in d'Antraigues' thought, his medievalism, which was already prominent in his first *Mémoire*.[4] His enthusiasm for the Middle Ages became later notorious. 'Let them call me madman,' he exclaims, 'a man of the twelfth century! Truly I would gladly exchange our customs for those of the age that is so scorned by our great wits, and our pretended virtues for the true virtues of the century which is so contemned. But, for my country, what I would desire are the immutable principles of the fourteenth-century constitution.'[5] In this way he comes finally to a definition of the *patrie* which reminds us both of Rousseau and of Burke. 'The *patrie* is in the union of the laws and the subjects as they have been modified by the laws; it is the manner of living, it is the safety of life and property; it is in the relations which one has established and

---

[1] *Quelle est la situation . . . ,* p. 60.
[2] *Exposé de notre antique . . . Constitution,* p. 13.
[3] *Réponse . . . à l'Auteur constitutionnel . . . ,* p. 102.
[4] *Mémoire sur les États Généraux,* pp. 87-90.
[5] *Lettre . . . à M. de L. C. sur l'État de France,* 1796, p. 10 n.

which have been formed around one.'[1] Possibly we can claim that even in his later years d'Antraigues' ideas are not to be entirely despised, although they had long ceased to have any political importance, if indeed they ever had any, save for his one brief, glorious moment of fame on the eve of 1789. Rapidly, as the revolution progressed, the force of circumstances, and one may perhaps add certain tendencies in the political philosophy he had inherited from Rousseau, led him to conservative conclusions, which the violence of his disposition and a life embittered by exile exaggerated into the extremest reaction.

When he perished miserably, assassinated along with his wife in 1812 by a dismissed lacquey, he had long sunk into obscurity. One cannot but feel regretful at the miserable fate of a man, endowed with considerable talent and generous enthusiasm, temperamental in the extreme, but capable of sincere affections, who had once stood on the pinnacle of fame, but in whose history circumstances seemed to have conspired with his character to bring about his ruin.

[1] id., pp. 16-17.

D'ANTRAIGUES MS.

. . . .

PARIS, 7, 7re, 1774

C'est en étudiant avec soin les mœurs de ces siècles si fortunés, si ignorans de nostre futile scavoir, si riches en sentimens et en sensibilité, que j'ai conçu que l'amour du pais natal était sûrement au-dessus de l'amour de la patrie et en différait sous tous les rapports. L'amour de la patrie est ce sentiment factice que conçoit un citoien pour son pais, qui pour lui est une patrie parce qu'il y jouit de ses droits d'homme et de citoien. Ce sentiment se compose d'amour pour sa patrie et de mépris pour tout ce qui lui est étranger. L'ambition, la gloire de sa patrie deviennent son ambition et sa gloire, son univers est l'enceinte de sa ville ou la frontière de pais. C'est là qu'il vit, c'est pour ce coin du monde qu'il veut vivre et mourir. Là est son existence, partout ailleurs se trouve pour lui un bannissement, un exil. Voilà ce que fut l'amour de la patrie pour les grecs et les romains.

L'amour du pais natal est plus naturel et moins héroique. En le considérant abstractivement, l'amour du pais natal existe partout, il ne connait aucun mode de gouvernement. L'amour du pais natal n'est autre chose que cette forte et indélébile reminiscence qui se grave toujours plus avant dans les cœurs pour les pais où se développèrent nos premiers goûts, nos premiers penchants, nostre première passion. Environnés d'appuis dans la tendresse de nos parens, de protecteurs dans tous nos voisins, d'amis dans nos contemporains, la première jeunesse se passe d'ordinaire au milieu d'une continuité de bienveillance, car l'enfant excite ce sentiment dans l'être le plus féroce, et l'enfant, n'inspirant ni jalousie ni méfiance, armé de toute son innocence et de son angélique sécurité, ne voit que des cœurs contents qui volent au devant de ses besoins. C'est dans ce doux état que naissent les premières illusions, ces illusions si décevantes mais si naturelles qui ne montrent partout que confiance et bonté, amitié et amour, bienveillance et sensibilité. L'enfant qui n'apperçoit que l'expression de ces sentimens, a-t-il tort d'imaginer que seuls ils règnent sur la terre. Il ignore qu'ils sont dus à sa faiblesse, à son impuissance, mais dès qu'il prendra sa place parmi les hommes il n'y trouvera que bassesse, mensonge et rivalité. Aussi à l'âge de l'experience est-il étonnant qu'il n'oublie jamais les rêves de son enfance, les illusions de sa jeunesse, et les pais où il en fut environné, que si ce fut auprès des lieux ou fut son berceau que son cœur sentit pour la première fois la soif d'aimer, est-il étonnant que le ciel sur la terre soit placé pour lui au lieu ou il en retrouva les délices?

Vainement il parcourut le monde. Les affaires, les inquiétudes, l'ambition, les calamités, l'ivresse du succès, tout le désabuse de ce monde qu'il parcourt en usant sa vie. Mais rien ne le désabuse de ses premières illusions; il s'y attache toujours davantage, il y tient par d'éternelles douleurs de les avoir perdues, il croit les retrouver dans les lieux ou il en fut abreuvé. Sa vie se passe à les désirer. Il faut les revoir. Il n'y retrouve plus les mêmes amis : la mort a moissonné les amis de son père et une partie de ses contemporains. Mais il y retrouve la même nature, les mêmes bois, les mêmes rochers. Ils lui rappellent tout ce qu'il éprouva, ils en furent les témoins. Son cœur tressaillit, ils deviennent ses seuls confidents; et n'aiant plus enfin d'ami que cette terre qui le vit naître il vient y chercher sa tombe, il lui semblant en y déposant sa dépouille confier son dernier secret à son plus vieux et à son meilleur ami.

Tel est l'amour du pais natal, plus naturel que l'amour de la patrie parce qu'il tient immediatement aux premières affections du cœur.

INDEX